AWAY WITH WORDS

Young Writers' 16th Annual Poetry Competition

It is feeling and force of imagination that make us eloquent.

How can I not dream while writing? The blank page gives a right to dream.

YoungWriters

Inspirations From Europe
Edited by Claire Tupholme

Young**Writers**

First published in Great Britain in 2007 by:
Young Writers
Remus House
Coltsfoot Drive
Peterborough
PE2 9JX
Telephone: 01733 890066
Website: www.youngwriters.co.uk

SB ISBN 978-1 84602 987 5

Foreword

This year, the Young Writers' *Away With Words* competition proudly presents a showcase of the best poetic talent selected from thousands of up-and-coming writers nationwide.

Young Writers was established in 1991 to promote the reading and writing of poetry within schools and to the young of today. Our books nurture and inspire confidence in the ability of young writers and provide a snapshot of poems written in schools and at home by budding poets of the future.

The thought, effort, imagination and hard work put into each poem impressed us all and the task of selecting poems was a difficult but nevertheless enjoyable experience.

We hope you are as pleased as we are with the final selection and that you and your family continue to be entertained with *Away With Words Inspirations From Europe* for many years to come.

Contents

The International School of Dusseldorf, Germany

The Poems

Journey

There's a long journey ahead,
We just started,
You are already dreaming
For it to be over,
But you don't even know
What our destination is . . .

Think again,
The journey isn't over yet,
There's much more to see . . .
When is it over?
Don't ask me . . .
Even people that have ended their journey
Are not capable of telling us . . .

Just think again,
Do you really want to arrive already?
Do you really want your life to be over?
Do you really want to be dead?

Malou Gunther (13)

Falling Memory

You are falling down.
Sinking down to nowhere
Like Alice in Wonderland

Whether someone pushes you
Or you
Naturally fall
If not
The time forces you to

You never feel how fast you go
How deep you go
And why . . . sometimes.
There is no ground under your feet.

Travelling in times,
You lose your eyes
That once charmed someone
You have no name
You have no face
Indeed your voice is gone
You finally have no shape,
While you do
You don't exist where you were

The fog comes
And wraps your nothingness
Like a spider ready for its meal.

You are existing
No more
In this world's mind.

Jihye Jeong (17)
Anglo-American School of Moscow, Russia

Letting Go

Emotions still run deep within her.
He keeps playing the same manipulative game
She knows she has to let go of him
Her friends all tell her that as well but she doesn't want to
                                                    listen to anyone.
She knows he's changed but she always thinks back, reminding
Herself of the guy he used to be.
The person who could look into her eyes and know how she feels.
The guy she used to love.
Valentine's Day was just another day for him and her,
They didn't need to prove or show they loved each other.
Every day was just another Valentine's Day.
Her biggest fear was losing him.
Now she's lost him, but she wants him to know she always wanted
Him to be happy
And he's not hers anymore but she'll always be there for him.
When she said I love you she really meant it
Her love will last forever
But she's taken everything that she could when it comes
                                                    to relationships,
And she can't take it anymore.
When she's gone maybe then he'll realise what he meant to her
And all the things she used to do
Because right now it really doesn't seem he cares.

Pooja Shah (16)
Antwerp International School, Belgium

Silence In The Forest

Dawn broke on the silent forest.
The birds awoke,
Their feathers fluttering.
Their chirping was heard far across the forest.
A hare poked its head out of its hole,
First one ear and then the next,
The sun was rising and so were the animals of the forest.

Like thunder and lightning,
Machinery worked its way into the forest,
Cutting and hacking.
And with a thump, thump,
Trees fell like dominoes,
Within a day 20 acres of forest was destroyed.

The night arrived,
The sun had set,
There was not a star in the sky,
Neither was there a living being in the forest.
There was silence.
Oh, that wretched silence,
Where not a single breath was heard.
The only thing that could be heard was the cold breeze,
The cold breeze on the brittle logs,
The cold breeze on the fallen leaves.

Where there were once living trees,
Now there were stumps.
Where one could see only green,
In the tree and leaves.
Now there was brown,
Twigs lay dead on the floor,
Stumps were scattered like gravestones in a graveyard.

The small streams which flowed through the forest,
Were red, with the blood of innocent animals,
What was once the lifeline of the entire forest,
Now carried the blood and bodies of the animals to their final
resting place.

The next day the machines would be back,
To destroy more of nature's beauty,
To rape Mother Nature again.

Armaan Parikh (15)
Antwerp International School, Belgium

Once Upon A Butterfly

Wings wipe clean eyelash sleep,
Her feet tingle-tangle in the breeze,
As dew dropped down on meadow plough,
Awakes sweet crystal-sized, tender eyes.

She butterfly kisses eastern sun rising,
Mosaic colours her wings aligning.
Honeysuckle flowers line the bank,
The day's audience calls her back.

From petal to pollen, her tiptoes glide,
Each moment rendered, from every menace she hides.
Flapping flying she dodges wild cats,
Their pitiless fangs like tree sapping bats.

Quick rest on a branch, a view of peace,
On lily pad sitting, takes a sip of a drink.
It is her flittering flattering partner, who makes her day,
And after her children are bred on safe side, she makes her way.

When Brother Sun and Sister Moon interchange in course,
Age like time, stars come peeping out.
No promise of tomorrow but life fulfilled to the brim,
Is what keeps Madam Butterfly away from feeling
The Reaper's dim grim.

Davene Le Grange (18)
Antwerp International School, Belgium

Diamonds In The Earth

I feel like I'm in Heaven
The storm is over now
Let's dance for a while
Before it starts again
Sooner or later we'll all be gone
Why don't we stay here for a while?
I'm sure you want to be forever young
Are you going to drop it now or not
Every month, every night
You are sitting on the same sandy beach . . .
Life is a short one . . .
We are like diamonds in the earth
But diamonds are forever and we are not
Can you imagine how the space would be
You don't have to worry for now
Enjoy your life here . . . in Greece.

Alkistis Romosiu (15)
Athens College, Greece

My Old Friend

My loyal old friend would be my parrot
Imagining him crawling for nuts
Would enjoy almonds very much.
Giving him patiencelessly Sunday's carrot.

I'd like him to stand proudly, on my right shoulder
Scratching my neck, showing joy
With his huge beak, always dry.
I'd never abandon him, there is no wonder.

However, ten years back, this emotionless canal was not chosen;
Now in my house there is not at all a cage,
Just my dog's house, within him and his quite big age.
And this was way more joyful than my dream,
The one forgotten.
My old friend . . .

Sergios Sofopoulos (14)
Athens College, Greece

I Have A Date

I have a date
It's in my dreams
It's in the mirror
It's in the air
It's every time
It's everywhere.

She comes to me
Her voice causes pandemonium heard from my chest
She is there, she's shiny, she's real
Her savoury perfume makes me feel ecstatic
Her smooth lips picture me Heaven
Her warmth lets me know there's nothing to compare.

But my date is cancelled
And I am still alone
Still a dreamer
Still in love
Still waiting
Forever.

Nick Campas (14)
Athens College, Greece

Decadence Poet

Modern drunken boat
In an old fading age
Sunken in his coat
With red snow in his cage.

Watching flowers dry
Wanting love and its rain
Letting out a cry
Hating life and its pain.

Dirty and alone
Shaping art of regret
Facing on his own
What the world will (soon) forget.

Aileezabeath Papadpoulos (14)
Athens College, Greece

So Sick Of Myself . . .

I'm so sick of myself
I'm just so ugly
Like something forgotten on a shelf
Something that people refuse to look at

I want to change but
Nobody is here to see me
Falling before I get up
Simply to go on with living

Nobody is here to catch me
While I'm falling
And I'm really falling
Without knowing why
It's simply happening . . .

I'm always so wrong
Nothing I do is right
I'm always hiding
I'm so afraid of others

I'm just so sick of myself
So tired of myself
But it's no one else's fault
It's just that everything is so wrong about me.

I don't know if I hate myself
But right now I'm tired
Tired of being myself
So sick of myself . . .

Christina Anthopoulou (14)
Athens College, Greece

Dawn

Darkness,
All he had known in his life
Shadows,
Hunting him
He could only imagine,
The ruby bright sun
For he'd only sensed its velvet warmth on his skin.

The emerald old cypress trees,
For he'd only listened
To the quiet murmur of their leaves
Dancing in the light breeze.
The beautiful flowers with their shimmery colours
For he'd only smelled their seductive fragrance
The vivid red strawberries
For he'd only tasted their sweet juice.

Desire and envy
Hope and disappointment
Desperation
Now he had at last the chance
To see, to enjoy
To live.
The pearly light blinded him for seconds
Then he saw
The sky was ashen, the landscape bare
After the raging storm
A rainbow, a hope
Sighing, it'll over
A nightmare.

Agelkiki Zeri (15)
Athens College, Greece

Miserable Minuet

It is pouring down
Washing away the dust
From the paths of my soul
Releasing pain and insecurity

Black gloomy clouds
Fill the corners of my mind
Until there is no space left

The soil is wet
As wet were my eyes
The day you mysteriously vanished

The sky is dark
As dark was the blood
Running down from your veins.

I keep telling myself
That I can still exist
Without you by my side.

But then why are you still
Haunting my dreams?

Why do I spend every day
Beside your grave

And why do I think of you
Every time the sky is filled with clouds
And the spirits begin to sing
Their most miserable minuet?

Anna Apostolopoulou (14)
Athens College, Greece

A Changeable Dream

The chain that holds me here, the fake idea
A place that we love, the piece that we lost,

The sensation of you,
Gone
Loneliness doesn't hurt anymore
Faith doesn't mean anything
We start a never-ending dream
We started as a team, we end alone
A whisper tells me that you wish to fly

A mirror broke, an angel fell
You whisper a spell, a hollow waking
We open our wings, but we can't fly
A lonely dream, that we can die
Mistake you say, mistakes we make

A scar on my cheek
A grudge in my heart
A rose's dreams
A demon survived

You whisper 'freedom' and I smile
This is my dream, to smile again
To touch the hopeless boy, and give him breath
To take a piece of my heart and share it

But dreams are dreams,
And reality hurts.

Ethimia Zachou (15)
Athens College, Greece

The Petrified Forest

It stood there, branches made of stone
No birds singing
No leaves rustling
Only grey cold stillness.

It was hopeless to wish
That rain would give it life.
Salvation could only come
If the sky took pity on the trees.

And then she comes along,
Full of rainbows and colours
Her pretty feet swept the earth
Her breath bringing scents
And oh, the miracle occurred;
The trees filled with blossoms.

Iro Spyropoulou (14)
Athens College, Greece

Arwen Undomiel

I looked down at the frozen land
And felt lonelier than ever before,
Dead leaves played games with the wind in front of my eyes.
In this land, I and my people used to live,
But now they are all gone,
And I am withering every day and every night,
More and more, until nothing from me will remain,
Until I become nothing but a shadow,
Until my days finish,
Until the end of the world.

Angeliki Taliouraki (14)
Athens College, Greece

Let Me Be Free

Let me be free,
Free from the hate, the anger,
The sickening feeling.

Stop judging me, I won't change,
I won't be like you, I won't listen, I won't understand,
I don't want to; you won't see who I am;
You want me to change, to be like everyone else,
Like the repeated verse, of a broken song,
It is not I who is different,
It is you, who stays the same.

I want a moment to be me,
But you will throw me down
You will break me with just a whisper,
You will tear off my wings and hide me from the sky,
You will take away my dream and crush it,
But I won't give you that pleasure.

Stop mocking me, you don't understand,
You don't listen, you don't want to,
Because of you my heroes are dead,
They died in my head.

I tried to help you become what you will never be,
Now take a good look at what you have done to me,
So let me go, leave me alone,
Let me be free.

Korinna Veropoulou (14)
Athens College, Greece

Silence

Bombing your ears with dust
Filling your heart with a void
Breaking your bones
Drying your throat.

Silence

It's louder than a crowd
The voice that tells you live, be, at least exist!
But it's louder than life
The emptiness inside you.

Silence

Emotion is not here
Thoughts are not here
You are not here
Only frozen tears running down two pale cheeks

And silence.

Tania Vassilikioti (15)
Athens College, Greece

All Alone

It's like nobody cares,
Can't they see me standing here?
I ask for help but they just pass by,
Sometimes I think it would be better to die,
I'm all alone, not a friendly face in sight,
The cold air hits me and it's soon night,
What's next? Where am I going to sleep?
Is this my life? Have I sunk this deep?
I'm all alone in the dark,
While I watch a new day start.

Maria Paalberg (13)
Birralee International School, Norway

The Ray Of Light

The light shines from the heavens above
It lights up my face
Makes me feel warm inside
Reminds me of friendship and love
Reminds me of spring
Rays of sunshine shining through the clouds
The year's first flowers on the wet grass
The first bee of the spring
The first day you can walk outside without a jacket,
Avoiding freezing to death
This is the time when fashion is in its high season.

Linni Sofie Tiller Ellefsen (13)
Birralee International School, Norway

Into The World Of Humans

How I prayed to be chosen,
Ahead of my yellow buddies,
I didn't want to rot for eternity,
Get out of this brown, labelled box,
Before my bumped, rotting neighbours,
And into the world of the plastic bag,
Get my sour juice squeezed onto the cooking food.
Then continue beyond the restricted bag,
Dare I go,
Into the world of humans?

Katrine Leine (13)
Birralee International School, Norway

The Wind

Help, my wind
You must
Not your icy blades today
How fast you fly
Into my soul
Cooling the love that
Tries to escape every day.

Juni Falck (13)
Birralee International School, Norway

Hope Of A Good Life

(Based on 'Prayer Before Birth' by Louis MacNeice)

I am not yet born; o save me,
Let the high winds guide me.
Let my mother's comforting grasp soothe me
And teach me how to be
When others are around me.

I am not yet born; o provide me,
With food to nourish me,
Clean air to refresh me,
Health to satisfy me.

I am not yet born; o protect me,
Let the strong man save me,
From the imprisoned or the undeserving.
Let no sinful creature come near me,
And fill me with tears of anguish.

Let no detrimental thing happen to me,
Otherwise take me, before I am born.

Benjamin Solt (16)
Brillantmont International School, Switzerland

Pre-Birth Plea

Make me not
Leave this comfy, warm place
With its constant flow of food
And beating rhythmic pace.

Force me not
To face the world
Whose inhabitants heave
And overcrowd.

Smother me not
To enter a world
That pushes to achieve
In things that I cannot.

Deceive me not
With well-intentioned lies
That convince all is well
But take me to Hell.

Cheat me not
Of my innocence
Let my childhood unfold
With gentleness untold.

Send me not
To war
To kill my fellow beings
But let us live in peace and healing.

Alex Power (15)
Brillantmont International School, Switzerland

A Prayer Before Birth Poem

O Lord, give me life,
To use and to play with,
To succeed and to convey with.

O Lord, give me experience,
To harden and educate me,
To give advice and to enlighten me,
To help others become part of me.

O Lord, give me strength,
To face my mistakes,
To protect those I love,
To better those I hate,
To see for myself,
The true errors of this race.

O Lord, give me freedom,
To succeed where I want,
To do what I will,
To find a way out
Of every bad spot.

O Lord, If nothing more,
Give me happiness, evermore.

Freddy Bossaerts (14)
Brillantmont International School, Switzerland

Questions

Nine months have passed, light at the end of the tunnel -
Will I be loved?
Will I be cute?
Will I be greeted in my birthday suit?
Will I be good
Or will I cry?
Will I be adopted without knowing why?

One year gone by, will I be learning to walk?
Another year later, will I be learning to talk?

Will I be treated with sweets and toys
Or will I be naughty and make a lot of noise?
Will I be good
Or will I be bad?
Will you smile to let me know you are glad?

Years gone by, am I in my teens?
Will I be good and eat all my greens
Or will I be bullied and fail in school
And will I be made out as the class dunce or fool?

I'm older now, have I made it this far?
Will I wear a suit and drive a fancy car
Or will I be a tramp and live in the streets
And will a few cents be considered a treat?

If I'm ever old and grey, it's such a long way away,
Will I take every day that I'm lucky to stay
Or will I end my life in grief
The way I began, with no hair or teeth?

John Fielden (15)
Brillantmont International School, Switzerland

Willing But Scared

I am scared to be born.
What if?
What if the world is empty?
I am scared to be born in a world of emptiness.
The world of emptiness is like an empty heart.

I am ready to be born,
If the world is,
If the world is full with love,
I am ready to be born in a lovely world.
The lovely world is like a beautiful flower.

I am afraid to be born,
What if?
What if the world is dark?
I am afraid to be born in a world of darkness.
The world of darkness is like a cloud blocking the beautiful sunshine.

I am willing to be born,
If the world is,
If the world is full of protection,
I am willing to be born in a protected world.
The protected world is like a child hiding behind their mother's back.

I am disappointed to be born,
What if?
What if the world is cold?
I am disappointed to be born in a world of coldness.
The world of coldness is like a turned off heater during the winter.

If I can choose
I am hoping to be born in a wonderful world,
If not, I prefer not to be born.

Emi Nakagawa (16)
Brillantmont International School, Switzerland

A Blue, Silent Death

In that sunny and dry July,
Glad and full of hopes,
Virgin and wild lands
Your fatal tomb.

It was your last day,
Your last mission,
Your last struggle.
Your passion betrayed you.
The steep rocks betrayed you.

With hope and burning tears,
You were brought to your Tirana,
Which gave light and brightness
To your past.

Grieving faces and white coats, tried their best
To stop the heavy blood from your salty wounds,
But you couldn't know,
You were sleeping in a coma's obscure world.
In the dazzling panic
They decided to send you to the close,
Overseas land of Apulia.

Quick was that cursed helicopter's departure,
You were five,
The pilot, the co-pilot, the engineer,
And your precious young son.
You never came back to the eagles' country.
Neither did the others.

Once again
The violent beauty of the sea
Exercised its brutal will.

The eagles mourned the five eagles,
Whose feathers were found a month later.

Juna Vuthi (16)
Brillantmont International School, Switzerland

Little Thoughts

The darkness surrounds me,
The unknown future scares me,
This fear doesn't leave me
Oh please, help me.

What will happen to me
If the world is cruel?
Who will I be?
How will I face fate's duel?
Oh please, protect me.

Love from within help me,
I hope I will be loved by the one
Whose soul will save me,
I know love might come to me.

I will have to leave you,
Because my mind will blossom,
Oh please, believe me
And finally forgive me.

Isabella Shamkina (15)
Brillantmont International School, Switzerland

Unborn

Here in my protective bubble
I can think of the troubles,
All the things in the world I do not know
I hope I'm protected and directed where to go.

I want a world that's entirely my own
I want to succeed so I become the strongest stone,
But there are others unlike me
That will get everything for free,
Who will never work a single day
And get their weekly pay.

Hopefully one day I will find my soulmate -
I hope I will be able to treasure our first date,
Or while I kick inside the womb
Am I just heading for doom?

Adam Kurth (14)
Brillantmont International School, Switzerland

Valentine's Love

The pain was too much to stand,
'Love her' was his heart's demand,
So he gave her his heart,
But she tore it apart
And his dream slipped away like sand.

Sam Green (15)
British School in The Netherlands, The Netherlands

The Room

A box
Filled with both literal and metaphoric
Hot air
Tens of little vulgar creatures
Leaving a trail of yoghurt pots
Pepsi cans and plastic bags
Wars being fought every minute
Over chairs, over effort, over girls.

Rational people have been lost
To its temptations.
The temptation of life, of people, of happiness
They come, thinking they can control it
But it controls them,
For they never realise
When it takes their soul
They no longer notice they had one.

Down the centre
Is an invisible line,
Showing the territory
Of the ruling class.
They control the sound,
They laugh and they jeer
Asserting their superiority.

Their subjects
Will one day be the ruling class
But they too
Will carry on the traditions
Of isolation, confusion and music
For they have lost their souls,
To this void

To embrace this room
Is to shun individuality
To shun diligence
To accept sloth, to accept greed
To accept pride

The air quivers
The noise is endless
It will hear an everlasting amount of forgettable, dull and crude
conversations.

It is the embodiment of human sin
It is what is wrong with humanity.

It's called a sixth form common room.

Jack Edge (16)
British School in The Netherlands, The Netherlands

Through The Eyes Of A Cockroach

I live in the cupboards,
In the walls and the floors,
Cracks in the corners
And holes in the doors.

I scuttle round tunnels,
Cobwebbed and faded,
I'm sick of these places,
So dark, damp and shaded.

When people see me
They shudder and squeal,
They don't really care
How that makes me feel.

They think I'm dirty,
A bug with no brain,
Flick me or squash me
Time and again.

I am a cockroach,
As great as can be,
I'm just as important,
If only you'd see.

Laura Dunbar (11)
British School in The Netherlands, The Netherlands

The Wanderer

Trailing crimson, He walks through a throng of humanity,
Laughing in the face of darkness' cold caress.
Eyes aflame, He hunts, safe in His insanity.

He knows your every desire; He toys with every fear,
Like a corpse dragging itself to its own funeral.
You scream in terror, yet closer draw near.

Wise man, evil man, madman, thief.
They call Him The Wanderer,
Hungry fingers reaching, your soul to reap.

He feels nothing, His heart callous as the abyss,
As He guides you to His house of horrors.
Like His suffering; bleed the pain that is His.

Smile like a jagged scar across a face of sin.
Abandon all hope ye who fall to His shadow,
Yield to despair that slams down like a guillotine.

He lives in shadows, quivering like an arrow into battle,
Waiting, crouched in dark that hides not His thirst.
A soft laugh, as your life slips away, rasping like a death rattle.

Wise man, evil man, madman, thief,
They call Him The Wanderer,
The dead one, with no soul to speak.

Beth Caradine (15)
British School in The Netherlands, The Netherlands

The Rebellion Of Toes

We are toes without a purpose,
But all that is gonna change.
Cos we feel it when you hurt us,
An' we're special, seem it strange.

We despise the way you stuff us,
Into shoes that stink to Heaven,
We detest the fact you use us
When you count to twenty-seven.

No longer shall you slap us
Down on dirty wooden floors!
Or stub us, come to think of it,
On tables, desks or doors.

But today, today so great will it be,
For today the head will fall
And now we are not down below,
We're fine and great and . . . tall!

We were toes without a purpose,
But all of that has now been changed.
No more can you hurt us,
'Cos we're special, seem it strange.

Nicola Kirby (12)
British School in The Netherlands, The Netherlands

Child's Nightmare

A sombre soul,
A fearful dream,
A nightmare that but one has seen.

The whistle of wind,
The whining of trees,
The floorboards that creak without a breeze.

I crept through a forest,
With a small green light,
That was a nightmare I once had to fight.

A luminous moon,
A black seashore,
A night with stars as no other before.

The grave of a man,
The dark omen close,
The wavering light without one to know.

This is the journey,
That no one has seen,
Apart from the child that once had a dream.

Caroline Haegeman (12)
British School in The Netherlands, The Netherlands

The Storm

The wolves have started running
Running through the air
Though our eyes are immune to see them,
We can feel them, they are there.

The wolves have started hunting
On this perfect day
Though the cubs are quite harmless,
The adults have come to prey.

Dancing, jumping, down and up
The wolves of the wind are like wind, they are wind
Coming, prancing, preying, dancing
Leaving nothing but the last bones of trees.

The wolves have come, the wolves have come!
The wind, the storm, the lightning blast!
The wolves have come and hid the sun
And scared away their prey.

The prey has hidden, the storm is passing,
The wolves are moving on
To the East they run, they howl,
But never forever gone.

The storm is a pack of howling wolves
Coming to feast in the windy plains,
They come, they go, forever returning,
Hunting through the flourishing lanes.

Anna Ruth Barton (11)
British School in The Netherlands, The Netherlands

Dark Night Prowler

Spending my days looking for something to eat
Spending my nights asleep on the street
Nobody cares
Yet everyone stares
Dog's hot breath against my feet.

Chased into a corner, against a brick wall
Tripping and stumbling, until I fall
Nobody cares
Yet everyone stares
Under their glares I feel so small.

A man with a metal charity tin
And wearing an RSPCA pin
Does care
And doesn't stare
But pities me and takes me within.

Warmth, food, love and sleep
No room to cry, no room to weep
Everyone cares
Nobody stares
And a family who take me home to keep.

Rosie Worster (12)
British School in The Netherlands, The Netherlands

Absolution

This is not what you hoped to become,
Introvert, deviant.
Soon you'll see the lies they've told,
Don't try to hold
Onto what you love;
It'll only be a matter of time
Before we learn the truth.
This delusion
We believe, is just some trickery,
Come on!
Pull the wool from your eyes,
And witness what we've become:
Fools for the pretence.

Let's not play the game,
Not be the same.
Androgyny, it seems
Is the key to the charade.
Can't you tell we're being had?
The clues are everywhere;
Scratches in the tapestry they wove,
The shame, to turn a blind eye.
So let's look beyond the smokescreen,
Clear its deception away,
Wipe away the stains of the times.

I'll ask only once,
Please, break from the chains
Stop them from softening the pain;
Shatter the rose-tinted glass,
And see,
Feel what it means to be free.

Christina Stimson (16)
British School in The Netherlands, The Netherlands

White Lie

Transferring miles into days,
I feel some kind of disgrace.
There's nothing wrong and neither right,
I don't know how to tell a lie.

I left her quarter past midnight.
A friend of mine was on my side.
I had a reason to be late,
But still I was a bit afraid.

Unlocked the door and took off shoes.
I wished I had some heavy booze.
She didn't notice how I came;
I stood behind and thought of blame.

Her smiling lips and shiny eyes . . .
I had to pay a bitter price.
And only now I understood
I didn't do the things I should.

She turned to me and smiled again
And now I got that she's a gem.
And it's too late to change my life,
But I'm not strong to tell a lie.

Dana Kibza (15)
College Alpin Beau Soleil, Switzerland

The Deepest Of Night

She was alone in the forest of her mind,
In the deepest of night,

The air felt mild but to her it was chilly,

And suddenly fear got to her,
And began to take over.

She started to weep,
And no one could hear her,

The hole in her heart was too big to fill,
And the knot in her throat was too hard to undo,

That thing that scared her was her own-self,

Reflected in a mirror of broken hopes
More perfect than ever,

It all went silent in a split-second,

At the end,
The knot was free and she stopped sobbing,

She had sank into that mirror of pain,

That lonely soul,
That hurting girl,
Was me.

Ivonne Sanchez (14)
College Alpin Beau Soleil, Switzerland

The Memorial

(Dedicated to all, dead or alive, who were fighting for
Estonia against Fascism during the Second World War)

Just tell me why,
Why do you dig the past,
When present is destroying future,
Does not allow our lives to last.

Just tell me why,
Why do you rub off fame
Of those who died for you and suffered,
Why do you need someone to blame?

Just tell me why,
You're forcing us to hate
Our loved and only motherland,
Which you now want to re-create?

Just tell me why,
You are becoming racist,
Towards your own, keen citizens,
Pretending they do not exist?

Just tell me why,
Why you abandon,
The ones who made you what you are now,
Choosing your heroes all at random?

Just tell me why,
When for you Russians pray,
You will eventually be puppets,
In paws of cruel USA?

Just tell me why,
Why you hear children cry,
By making them forget their grandads,
Who gifted us the bright blue sky?

The signs from bullets, tears and scars,
Light up the flames of goodbye stars.

Anna Kornilova (14)
College Alpin Beau Soleil, Switzerland

Full Stop (.)

I was once seeking Him, the so called One but rather Three.
Found Him I have but . . . found He remained as the Prophet dictated.

Love, greed, guilt, and all the fictional feelings, mock me!
Their experience darkens the self - which self?!
Cold I stand - as one forever has been
Ignorant; indifferent and above all, selfless and doubtful of him.

Reborn was I, was I?
Through darkness I walked
Nothing found, I never shall as my will forbids, for chained it is.
O Death! Crawling past . . . me,
Ignoring as I ignore,
Deceiving as I deceive,
Outsmarted I was,
And so I remained, 'Remained I have not!' - (claims the Prophet)

The . . . end! The disastrous end!
Showed itself, presumed I so and right I was.
Horrifying it was not, never will be
Deceived me He has, as well!

Lurking around through the hazy fortress,
I wove my thoughts around a decision:
Stop! O Master, I pledge to thee my inner Prophet.
And stopped all was
And so it remained: forever!

And all that was true - or not! - (the prophet shouts)
Forsaken became, disappeared . . . at once!
Why? Why not? - (insists the prophet)
Deserved it I had, deserved it we had
Ignored remained I, ignored became thee
Ignored will be I and so will thee
Eternally: Black!

Placinta Razvan (16)
College Alpin Beau Soleil, Switzerland

Untitled

Of all the days the brightest
Light poured from the deep blue west
And though, sorrowful event,
My sight is insensitive to laughter.

Hardly you were living, whimsical sick owl
How could blindness leave me lifeless, drive me away?
Hardly you could bear me, blameworthy criminal
Hated me, poison of your joy,
Never ceased to love you more each day.

But the sentence fell at last, shall lay you still in your grave,
Your eyes shut forever, dark bed of forgetfulness,
Peace shall grow on your place.

Tears shall drown the wrath and feed the memorial
Sleep, Pride's victim, get away from the madness,
Rest in peace, my dear friendship;
My beloved essential.

Deborah Schneider-Luftman (17)
College Alpin Beau Soleil, Switzerland

Grandfather

A blank
Left
Where you were

Left
To be filled

Waiting
Wasn't necessary

Clashes of colour
Cacophony of sound
The world

And it was gone,
Gone,
Gone,
Gone,

You away
Me here

No memory
No reminiscence
No nothing

Only
A wisp of your name
Hidden,
Buried,
Trampled,
Under a patchwork of
The world
Touches me

Suddenly,

Suddenly.

Young-Hee Kim (17)
College Du Leman, Switzerland

Desert Nights

Flowing wind, so blessed, a heartbreaking glance
Dancing feet on the sand, this is my only chance
Over the mountains, came with fights
So much for the desert nights.

Here she comes, such a glamour
Soft cloth, lavender breath, on the sand, tilts her head
Long hair curtains, eyes closed tight
Deep into the desert night.

Such a world, no one can cry
Enchantment of the desert, keeps you high
Silence broken by unearthly sounds
So happy at the desert nights

This is a different paradise
A man's armour, a woman's jewels
Black eyes looking cold as ice
The everlasting paradise, desert nights.

Dark sky, the amazing tune
Dresses glittering, distant voices chanting
Musical magic, charms in an ancient rune
At the desert nights, beautiful face shining.

She looks back, shooting my heart
Says in this world, we all play a part
Party continues, the curtains flow
My heart longs for a desert night.

Kardelen Kala (16)
English High School for Girls, Turkey

Lost Loves

When the time starts
Loves were pure, thoughts were pure
Then the years had passed
Time had gone
Taking our loves, taking our thoughts.

Then the tears had come
Ruled by the pain
Made us strict
More and more in the time
We changed a lot
Losing humanity
Unable to talk, unable to share.

Rivers between us
Apart from sides
We all turned inside
Avoid having broken hearts
Living with the lonely hearts
We thought safe, it was
Too blind to see
It was breaking us.

Now unconsciously
Asking our hearts
'Where we lost the love?'
Searching for it everywhere
Except our hearts
Without knowing
It is waiting for us
Right into our hearts
And by the time we look there
We will find it looking into our eyes.

Lerna Untur (17)
English High School for Girls, Turkey

Nature In My Eyes

The most pure and most innocent place
Like a child's smiley face

A place to hide
A friend by your side
As a daily protection
Where you need love and affection

Where to play, have fun
Jump around, throw a ball
Hide-and-seek, find them all
Enjoy yourself, no judgements none.

In each season, for a different reason
In the light or in the dark
Whether it's raining or snowing
Gloomy or glowing
Or it's the light that crosses our sight.

Reflect, think about every situation
There won't be any hesitation
Go on and show a demonstration
Just like any other imitation.

All the green and leaves that fall
Insects, animals that crawl
The many different creatures
Gives it magical interesting features.

It is different for every one of you
That is what it makes the enchantment true
It's magic, it's a dream
Express yourself, shout and scream
One of the treasures to hold
The pleasures are as you are told.

Ludovica Tassinari (12)
International School of Trieste, Italy

Autumn Poem

It was a cold, sunny, autumn day,
Leaves were falling down their way,
The path of flowers all grey,
Nearly like a winter day.

People enjoy all their free time
Playing kids in the sunshine,
Suddenly they just frowned,
Raindrops bouncing down.

Babies crying,
Nappies flying
Suddenly it was clear,
On the path where it was grey
Just a little baby dear.

Leaves were falling, soft as snowflakes,
Red and yellow, gold and brown;
The breeze laughed creepily from the treetops,
Shaking all the colour down.

All joined hands and circled round
While we watched the leaves fall down
See them twirling to the ground,
See them dancing all around.
See them skipping here and there,
See them flipping in the air.
Autumn leaves so peacefully,
Falling, falling from the tree.
Where was I?
In my bed?
Was it just a dream?
The path was normal and had bright-coloured trees.

Djamal Fateh (13)
Morna International College, Spain

The Crazy Horse

There was a horse called Perla.
She was as crazy as a spinning wheel.
No matter how she would feel.
Sad, happy or even not feeling well
Crazy kicking and rolling on her feet
That's was what she liked, like hell!

But one day she didn't eat
Not even biting on her treat.
There was something wrong
Running hard didn't take long.
Her owner was on a holiday
Somewhere far far away.

Maybe it was the food, maybe the drink
No one could find the secret link.
Her breath was hot and she was sweating a lot.
There was no owner so she stayed like a loner.
But then the stable boy had an idea
He would call the owner, and say Perla was a bit weird.

So that's what he did.
The owner came back a bit concerned
But when Perla saw her she had no comment
All of a sudden she became wild again
She wasn't anymore the sick Zen
Now they knew how she felt
She just missed her owner, was that what she meant?

Charlin Ooms (13)
Morna International College, Spain

Bully

I get to school, I go to class.
I'm late again. Mum drank too much and broke a glass.
Through lessons I get told off. I don't work enough.
But instead of crying I act tough.
I get home and my parents fight.
Dad says Mum is crazy, I hate him but he's right.
He leaves home, leaves Mum, leaves me.
I can't think, I cry, so does she.
But then she gets the bottle, it helps her forget.
Her pain will get worse after, I bet.
Next morning I get to school
All these happy kids make me feel like a fool.
A big green monster called Envy catches me.
I hate those kids, it's them who I want to be.
Why should they be happy, when people like me exist?
My eyes fill with tears, which cover them like mist.
Hate covers my heart, burning, stinging
In my ears revenge keeps ringing.
On the way home I see a happy kid wearing glasses.
His little toy shines in his hand as he rushes.
I stop him and swear at him. I break his toy.
Tears leak out of the stupid boy.
He cries for help and Mummy.
His pain screams while I punch his fat tummy.
I drop him down on the hard floor.
I feel great as I make him sore.
I leave him there to bleed. I walk away.
It's his fault for being happy when people have such bad days.
When I get home nothing has changed at all.
It's all the boy's fault, next time I'll really make him fall.
I'm a bully, I don't care,
The world is just so unfair.

Costanza Chiavari (12)
Morna International College, Spain

The Letter

There was once a king who knew no better
Than money and throne 'til the impolite letter

Or so it had seemed to the king that day
As the butler read out in a very calm way

'You foul, unfriendly, spoilt little man'
The letter had read, 'You don't give a damn!'

'Just a minute,' said the King who was starting to fret
The butler continued, the King was upset.

'Stop now!' the King ordered, 'I demand you to!
Find me that man! It's him I will sue!'

But the butler did not stop, instead he read on
Until the King's selfish anger had gone

The final lines of the letter were these
Words of wisdom, the writer's pleas.

'Now I do not mean this in anger or aggression
Instead I just wish for you to make a confession

And for you to be kind and loving to others
And treat the world just like they're your brothers.'

Daisy Veale (12)
Morna International College, Spain

Football

F is for friendship, you play in a team
O is for opinion, could the ref be so mean?
O is for offside, the flag waved up high
T is the tackle, you're sent off 'goodbye'
B is the ball, the poor thing, kicked all over the place
A is the people who all play, free of hate and of race
L is for legs, they kick the ball hard
L is for lazy, which I'm not, so let's go have football fun.

Ben Hartmann (13)
Morna International College, Spain

The World And Pollution

If the world bothers you show it pollution
If pollution bothers you show it hippies
If hippies bother you show them the seventies
If the seventies bother you show it the Vietnam War
If the Vietnam War bothers you show it the Americans' retreat
If the Americans' retreat bothers you show it healthy food
If healthy food bothers you show it sweets
If sweets bother you show them salt
If salt bothers you show it goats
If goats bother you show them a butcher
If a butcher bothers you show him a vegetarian.

Bene Andrist (11)
Morna International College, Spain

Thoughts

I'm trying to make myself clear
Why work for our lives,
When there's not going to be a tomorrow,
Poles will melt, the earth will sink,
Underneath the barriers of water.

Why work to be the best lawyer in the world,
When you may appear dead in bed.
The world of today,
May be nothing for the world of tomorrow.

Marcos Ribas-Hazell (14)
Morna International College, Spain

Valentine's Day

Valentine's Day falls on a day of the year
When it's cold and grey,
But as if by magic everything seems
To be more colourful and love is in the air.

But somewhere in this world is war even today.
On that day my heart is full of love
And if the rest of the world would feel the same
At least on that special day
There would be no war.

Laura Gassen (13)
Morna International College, Spain

The Encouragement Behind

Although it's not the biggest thing,
It does play a big part in some of the most important things.
It wraps over all those negative factors, and opens
Many positive.

It doesn't matter for anyone
Apart from the one it applies to,
That person would be the owner of this encouragement behind all,
And do the task without struggle.

If you are handed this power
Or not
It depends on what you do,
What you like and who you are.
You could be given the encouragement to do things people would
Never imagine seeing or doing.

Things otherwise looked on as burdens and extra work could be
Looked on as challenges and excitement.
There is nothing better than feeling great in what you are doing.
This power will give you the will to continue.

Julian Hisdal Nymark (15)
Oslo International School, Norway

Misty Formosa

In the smoky old days
On a sunny morning
Red hair beast thumping around our mother land
Taking over
Destroying
Invading from a foreign land.

True

In the smoky old days
On a sunny morning
People from the far west
Sailing across the Pacific
Giving our name
Formosa

In the old smoky days

A dark black cloud came floating in
Crows start singing
Children running home to seek sanctuary
The black omen has showed itself

Thieves
Pirates
Armed soldiers
Invading from the north
Ruled our land over half a century.

Left.

The sun shining over our faces
The sound of children's laughter
The clouds faded
Crows flew away
The dark days are over
Then a new mist roamed over the land.

Yu-Jung Liu (15)
Oslo International School, Norway

City Of Blinding Lights

Sleepless nights for the animals at the zoo
    Why?
Because of our everyday lives
Traffic from day till night and night till day
    Beep, bang, crash
There is no stop to this noise.

The brightness they see every night isn't from the calm moon
Or even the shining stars but from a city of blinding lights.

    Shut away from their wild life
Stuck in this hell within a cage dividing them from life beyond these
    Prison bars
Laughter from children, amusing for kids
But do you ever think is it amusing for these animals?

Take a minute and study the cute fuzzy faces of the animals
    But this time, look beyond the grin
A sad story lays behind that misleading smile
A story of a cruel capture from the wild
    The family tie was broken forever for these animals
Shut away from their freedom forever . . .

But in this zoo within a city of blinding lights
    Their nature is reversed
In this zoo they are enclosed from their real life until they die slowly
    And forever forgotten.

Samia Chaudhari (15)
Oslo International School, Norway

The Moving Train

If you can remember
The good times you've spent
You'll probably realise
How fast they went.

Imagine all the good friends
That have gone to waste
Like a really sweet chocolate
With a bad aftertaste.

Like a train passing by
In the middle of the night
Hard to see at first
Because it's so bright.

And on the train
Through the window
You can see the people
As they come and go

And then you see a face
So pretty you'll want it to stay
Even though you realise
The train will soon take her away

So what's the point of having
All those good friends?
Or spending those good times
If they're just going to end?

This is the question
It is always the same
Then I see the light
Of the next train.

Kyle MacLeod (14)
Oslo International School, Norway

Ignorance

A child, ignorant to bone
Accepting of all
No questions asked
No response given
Perfect tool of power

But soon it grows

It is no longer ignorant
It understands
It has been betrayed
It lashes out upon the power

It is now He
No more it

He is a power of powers
He understands more
He is wise
The realisation occurs
Keeping those in power
No questions asked
No response given
Perfect tool of power

But then the day
Day when it comes
Just as he did before

And he wishes,

That he had stayed ignorant.

Doug Welsh (15)
Oslo International School, Norway

The Red Hope

The farmhouse walls are mouldy and dark
The animals skinny and weak,
They are all seeking
For the better end,
Lifestyle,
Housing
And peace.

The red day comes,
It shines light on the farm
Hope for us all,
Its slogan-bread, peace land,
This must be life.

The papers told
It all so well - life is good
It is a fairy tale.

Outside my window
The story does not match.
All is not well,
Not at all.

Still the papers say
It's all just a phase,
We will just have to wait
But it is worse than before.

The farmhouse walls are rotted and gone
The animals dying and weak.
We all need
The better end,
Lifestyle,
Housing
And peace.

Øystein Walderhaug (14)
Oslo International School, Norway

No Life To Live

Bliss, Heaven, joy,
The angel's best,
Crystal eyes,
Tiny hands,
God's child,
Her soft porcelain skin,
Mine to love and cherish.

Anguished, unwanted, despondent,
A weed among flowers,
Smack! Bang!
Black rings, grey eyes, bruised face,
She had become a lonesome child,
No friends, no family, no love,
No life to live.

Love them, they need you.
Support them in what they do.
You can help build the future.
Do you want a world
Weeping
For love?
A bleak
Woebegone
World of hate . . .
Then devote yourself to them,
They are humans,
And they are the
Future.

Alexandra Vernon (15)
Oslo International School, Norway

Purpose Street

This sunrise.
Wearing his only trousers and dishevelled hair,
Jude went to Purpose Street
Where he'd appointed a fortune teller
In which he believed.

> The very same sunrise.
> Jack, in his freshly ironed suit and combed hair of gel,
> Had arranged to meet a future predictor
> In whom he believed.

Excitement rising within him,
Jude tapped his fingers on his knee,
The subway was almost there,
A place beyond his lifestyle.

> Jack tried to lean back in the taxi,
> On his way to Purpose Street,
> Before his life would be revealed,
> For so far, money hadn't bought him love.

> Jude was
> Shy,
> Thankful,
> Thoughtful.

> Jack was
> Timid,
> Grateful,
> Considerate.

The same future the teller predicted, the same life they both
went through.
Yet in two different worlds.
To say that they were soulmates would not really be untrue.
But chance had by chance separated them in diverse worlds.

Martine Groven Hoffmann (14)
Oslo International School, Norway

The Government Totally Sucks

Maybe it's not too late to forget how to hate
To learn how to love and forget all the pain
Maybe some day we could do right
Instead of always doing wrong

Just to look around
Hurts down inside
Will they fix my broken bones
Or will I bleed forever?

How do they sit there
Ignorant to everything
Except for the money?
They feed us their lies and their b*******
They talk down on us
What the f*** is wrong with them?

Someday they're gonna fall
From their mighty power wall
And we'll be there
To spit on their lowlife faces
And return the power to the people!

Only then will we realise
The errors of the past
And only then will we erase
The horrors of the past.

Louis Curran (14)
Oslo International School, Norway

There He Walked . . .

He walked and walked, not giving up his path
Unlike other people who would've given up already,
He never bent his knees and never grieved.

He walked and walked, not giving up his path
His motion of walking was the same as usual,
Pushing other people in his way, listening to no one.

He walked and walked, the same way as usual,
Although he had achieved nothing
He walked and walked, but suddenly stopped, until he understood
                                            something,
Others were able to see more than he was,
Every day, every week, every year, the distance between him and
                                            them getting further,

He understood, the path he had chosen, was wrong,
And education is the best weapon a human can have
Soon he changed his mind to take another path,
But the path he had abandoned before, was now a cliff,
No longer needed to be walked, but to be climbed.

Therefore he grieved and cried in regret,
For the meaningless hours he had spent,
And the waste of energy he had to use to keep going on his path.

But he soon started to climb the cliff in happiness,
Since he had already learned something valuable.
He will keep climbing, although the cliff is so steep,
In hope that he will have a new future.

Jae-Ho Kwak (15)
Oslo International School, Norway

Trouble Sleeping

I toss and turn
In my bed
As thoughts
Bound through my head
My sheets
Tangle up under me
Why
Can't I just be free
Breathing is heavy
And strong
Nights are cruel
And long
Watching the clock
Move
What have I got
To prove
Time moves
Like a slug
I sigh
With a deep shrug
My heart pounds
With grief
Knowing
There's no relief
Fists clench
With frustration
All I need
Is some concentration
Thoughts
About many things
Float about
With tiny wings
Hours pass
With no stop
My hope
Of sleep was a flop
I just need
A little sleep

Even
Just a minute peep
It shouldn't be
This tough
It shouldn't be
This rough
It's not hocus-pocus
I just need
To focus
It's time
To rest now
But I don't know
How
My eyes heavy
Like stones
I can finally rest
My bones
A nice calm
Takes me
Over
I've finally
Found
My four leaf clover
No more
Stress
I've sorted
Out
The mess.

Erika Sagert (14)
Oslo International School, Norway

The End Of The Grey Mountain Vixen

The taste of sheep was still prominent in her mouth,
The smell of raw flesh still in her nostrils.
The comforting music of the cubs
Along the clucking of the stream.
The day seemed perfect.
The pack was sleeping,
Content
In the morning sun.

Then they came,
Helicopter sounds across the valley
Barking at her cubs
Telling them to hide
She rushed through the clearing
Taste of blood in her mouth
Panting
Swishing through the pines

The snow
Crushing, breaking beneath her paws
The unknown fear
Behind
Closing in
Tattattattatta
Smell of humans
Chasing her through the forest

Pang!

'My puppies!'

Silence . . .

Just puppies weeping

Then . . .

Nothing

But the Grey Mountains cried for her
and the arrogance of the people.

Knut Lembach-Beylegaard Berg (16)
Oslo International School, Norway

The Bride

My eyes open after four years of coma sleep
I sit up straight and gasp for breath, clutching my head
Screaming, I reach for my stomach which feels so bare. I start to weep
Where's my little baby girl? Or was I just dreaming?

My memories are gone. Where am I? How did I get here?
I silently cry as the cold black creeps in . . .
I remember now. Memories of pain and fear
Now everything is red. A representation of both blood and death. Sin

My wedding day and everything, beautiful, white and clear
A fiancée who loved me and our coming baby
There was happiness and no smell of fear
I could have changed what happened, maybe

All that white went red, when Bill came
Bill killed them all . . . even they tried to kill me
Now nothing will be the same
There was so much blood . . . on my dress, in my face,
I could barely see

I lay on the church floor angry and sick,
Bill stood over me with a gun. My white dress now covered in blood
I looked into the barrel of the gun
Pain and darkness hit me like a flood.

Thinking of what he did would drive anyone but me into madness
Sitting in this place
Shaking with anger and sadness
Even though my head is still in space . . .

One thing is certain in my mind, he took my little baby girl's life . . .
The thief
There is one thing I still have, my speciality which is to kill
That is what I want to do to all those assassins and for an end
to this grief . . .
I will kill Bill

After all I was once told . . .
That revenge is a dish best served cold.

Monique Burvill (14)
Oslo International School, Norway

It Was Me!

My boyfriend,
My best friend;
Loved ones,
Backstabbers!

I cared for them!
Somehow, I got lost;
Thinking they cared for me as well,
Everything was lies!

I didn't think it would come down to this . . .
Lying, like men in poker games.
Now, they're gone!

Arguments;
That's how it began.
I couldn't take it anymore!
It was my turn . . .

'Revenge!' is what I like to call it,
Sweet;
Spiteful;
Satisfying revenge!

They made me suffer!
Day after day,
Night after night . . .

I act heartbroken;
As if I'm lost;
Sad and helpless;
The others see me like this,
Because, I hide a deep secret!
I did it! I killed them,
Those backstabbers!

Samantha Jeffries (14)
Oslo International School, Norway

Innocent Baby Girl

Memories, horrible memories
So bad she was up all night
Screaming and crying
Nightmares with no end.

She gets hit in her face
She gets kicked in her ribs
They used her like a punching bag
It looked like a red balloon that burst over her
Oh, my innocent baby girl
Their desire to destroy someone's life.

My innocent baby girl
Walking peacefully alone
With no suffering or pain in sight
Oh, my innocent baby girl

Two white men
Drinking till they can no more
Madness in their small pebble eyes
Only wishing to satisfy their drunken minds

Bruises all over she had
She looked soulless and beaten up
They couldn't have beaten her up no more

Because of those two white men
I won't have no grandchildren
A fierce pain pierces through my gut
Every time I think about it

Damn, those two white men
Revenge shall be mine.

Karl Fredrick Hiemeyer (14)
Oslo International School, Norway

Don Quixote

I am a knight errant from La Mancha
My quest is to fight enemies and to save my love
Her name is Dulcinea del Toboso
Her eyes are like shining stars in the sky
And her hair is like Indian silk
She is delicate and tender like a butterfly
And I'm coming to redeem her
I am accompanied with my friends,
Squire Sancho Panza and
My loyal horse Rocinante
There is a great deed to be done,
I must defeat a powerful enemy,
It's a ferocious wind-making giant.
I charge my enemy
The mighty giant hits me like a thunder
I fall on the dried-up ground
Sanch Pancha runs up to me
I tell him
Even though I'm dying,
I defeated the enemy,
Now I can die.

Tomas Jablonskas (14)
Oslo International School, Norway

Jo

Indoctrinated
I buried it in the backyard
My stories, my talent
Like a mole without legs, it lay in the soil
With the spade in my hand, shaking off the toil.

My glistening hair grabbed around my neck
I am a miserable crow, what have I got left?
The sun licking my skin, lifting my head
The spade lying there
A relief

One question lingering, why be a puppet?
My hands itching to grab the handle
The ground pounding the grass a-tangle
Like a dog I struggled through roots and stones
As I grabbed the muddy book a shiver spread through
My bones

The dear one clenched tightly in my arms
Like two jigsaw pieces completed in my palms
I am back to being me again Jo,
Just Jo.

Emily Gretland (15)
Oslo International School, Norway

Bob Marley

'Come on and smile'
'You're in Jamaica yo'
Growing up in
Kingston's ghetto
An inspired musician
With no education
Soon to discover
Greater things
'I smoke two joints in the morning'
'I smoke two joints at night.'

Rastafari lead me to
Smoking herb
'Herb so good for everything'
My great care for my dreads
'Natty Dread'
Greater music talent
All for the better
My career went forward
My love for herb grew
'Herb, herb is a plant'
As well as my love for music
'Catch a fire.'

During my success
I had what
Every musician has,
A downfall
'Bad boys, bad boys
What you g'na do, what you g'na do
When they come for you?'

I will always
Be remembered
As a
Legend
'Exodus;
Rebel
Soul Rebel'

Freedom Fighter
'Buffalo Soldier'
God
'I shot the sheriff'
Musical genius
Jammin'
That is me
Robert Nesta Marley
(Bob Marley)

Carl-Jacob Wahlstrom (15)
Oslo International School, Norway

The Cold

So abnormal,
This feeling.
Pain and misery
Magnified
A hundred times.
Perhaps the fact that this is not a fatal disease
Like
Lung cancer or AIDS or heart disease or influenza
Or pneumonia or or or or
Or . . .
Or.

Maybe this little pain - a change, a difference
Gives us room
Gives us time
To allow ourselves
A little self-pity.

Kaitlin Huynh (14)
Oslo International School, Norway

Beast

Clenching,
Claws of diamond,
Jaws of stone.
I am a ragged, lost boy,
Turned from myself,
A stranger in my body.

A vulture scared of heights,
Suffering, trapped,
In a rotting world . . . wrapped

All they feel, in a wealth of fear:
Terror, disgust, distrust,
And all they say, crisp and cold:
Who cares for a beast?
Shaggy and old.

And all I think:
Not one.
In their wild ecstasy.

Kirsty Coombs (14)
Oslo International School, Norway

Marianne Dashwood

I am lost and confused,
Why would he do this?
We had ultimate happiness ahead of us
But he abandoned me, like an old dog.

The pain he has caused me is unexplainable,
It's like having a knife stabbed straight into the heart.
It doesn't go away, it doesn't die
The cut just bleeds.

It's like a thick layer of ice that has covered my heart,
Turned into cold since my sunshine has faded.
The aching is so vigorous that it burns,
Like my insides are being eaten by blazing fire.

I have lost control,
There is not a muscle on my body I can handle.
I am no human any longer,
I have no craving for nourishment,
No desire to sleep.

All my sense is gone,
Except the sense to suffer.
It's an illness with no antidote
A never-ending torture

The desperation to see him,
Feel his touch, his kiss, his warm embrace
To be closer to him in any way,
Even just a short breeze of his scent

Look at my face
Eyes are red, face stained with tears,
Bawling my eyes out . . .
I plead for his return.

But no . . . he has reached into my heart,
Gripped it tightly with his bare hands,
Ripped it out . . . showing no remorse
And left me there, breathless
To drown in my own weep.

Siri Conesa Holmeide (14)
Oslo International School, Norway

For Real, Tupac

A troubled child in criminal cases
A confused youth wandering round bad places
Rolling with fellow thugs
On the street, smoking and selling drugs.
It was the cops with the racist faces

She raised me without my papa
I still do love my mama
I am where I am today
'Tis not her who should have to pay
For 'tis I that started the drama

I made you shed tears
Never meant to bring all those fears
Yeah I know it was hell
Was hugging you from a jail cell
Sorry for all those years

Music's my portfolio
Kicking back in the studio
A message to all my fans
Let's march together with joined hands
I tell them to keep it real
And that it is love they must feel

Connected them through rap
Could I have missed a gap?
What happened at last gig
Man, I acted like a pig
Mad and out of control
Like a demon in my soul

On stage and lost my cool
Challenging fans for a duel
Shall never forget that day
Everything was not okay
I wish I could take it back
For that may be the last of Tupac.

Julius Faenoe (15)
Oslo International School, Norway

They've Returned

(Feelings of Andrew Wiggen at the end of 'Speaker for the Dead'
by Orsen Scott Card)

Hated by all
Yet loved by all
What I did,
Who I killed
Unaccountable numbers
Yet only a few individuals
They made me
And they'll make me
Do it again
They ordered it,
Deceived me to do it,
Told me that
It was just a game
Afterwards,
I learned what I did
I cried for the
Billions killed, in the
Name of humanity
And I told
Everyone about them
Under a different name
The most loved
Turned into the most hated
But I brought them
Back from the dead
And no one knows it,
All wishing that
They were alive,
Only while they are dead.

Matthew Stevens (14)
Oslo International School, Norway

The Street And The Beggar

The asphalt is my closest friend
My poor spine aching from sitting bent
I want to lift my head
But the hateful gazes of the passers-by pains me even more

I hold a cup no one else uses
Wear rags no one else wants
I have a bag full of belongings no one else needs
But to me they are important
The old red blanket; a happy memory
And three rusty coins

Could you spare a coin? Drop it in the cup?
No, I'm scum in their eyes, an old worthless weak man
I wish I could find
Someone's whose mind
Could understand how my life really is

Hateful gazes
Because of my rags? That I smell?
Seems that they hate me
Why? They don't know me

Could you give me some money?
No . . . they want expensive honey
I'd like to buy my first shirt
But how to make money when they think I am dirt

Trapped inside an evil circle
Those outside seem so fickle
They have the boat,
But still they won't help me over the deep moat

I look at the street
It is always there
I always know where
It always offers a spot
Not into the annoying lot

The street, my only friend.

Konrad Holtsmark (15)
Oslo International School, Norway

Queen Of The Nile

My seductive smile known to beset and beguile
The leaders of Rome,
Is my Modus Operandi.
Coal black hair and kohl-black eyes
Paint my face
Mona Lisa of the Nile.

My father's death shadows the sundial
Flash, I am queen, but soon squeezed out.
My anger assembling armies in Alexandria.
With battle clashes and butterfly lashes, I seize Caesar's heart
And Egypt's throne with my seductive smile.

I clamp his heart with jaws of a crocodile.
Blinded by love, I am his addiction
Like a moth to a flame.
My red balloon is stabbed with that same crimson knife,
Both lover and love lasted only a short while.

How many times must I walk down the aisle?
Mark Antony. Bewitched by my beauty and imprisoned by my charms,
New lover, husband, father
Together we rule. Triumph and defeat.
Until my last sad smile.

Flashing before me is my life in exile
In the reflection of the puce poison vial
Who do I see?
Queen of the Nile.

Bridget Fitzgerald (15)
Oslo International School, Norway

Healing Wound

Sitting
Reliving
It all began back then,
I remember

Settling where we were, was no option, no way
Choking on the need for renewal, seeking love I suppose
Moved on now, we're here, somewhere new
Will we stay?
For good? Who knows?

My little girl and I, we were the news
The citizens' suspicions so present, so tranquil
The scepticism and the shrews
The 'welcome' sounded so hostile

Before him, it was all dark, so dim
He's the light in my abyss
Water in the drought
I love the taste of his kiss
No doubt

It took so long, to feel alive again
To smile and mean it
But now I know the wound will heal
Now I know, this is for real.

Athina Kefalopoulos (15)
Oslo International School, Norway

Jimi Hendrix

This was a dream
Things change
People change
Music changes
Weed, women and booze
I feel the music
I let the vibrations run through me
Each note an inspiration
Sad songs like daggers in their hearts
I feel the guitar
It talks to me
Manic depression is taking my soul

Each solo and bend of a string
Sending me into a cosmic trance
People around the world worship me
Respect me
Want to be me

Woodstock
Last day
I slowly step onto the stage
It sends me through the clouds

The blues run through me
Like a midnight freight train

My final day
Lived out in peace
Constant drinking almost comforts me
Peacefully asleep
Choked on my vomit
I am no more.

Callaway Williamson (15)
Oslo International School, Norway

The Traveller

I have been everywhere,
To places I have no care,
Even the cold and bare.

I have set foot in Georgia,
As well as Nova Scotia,
Even old Russia.

I can live in a castle far away,
As I can live in any way,
But I miss you more and more every day.

I know you're somewhere out there,
Just don't know where,
I wish I did, 'cause I care.

Every day I'm somewhere you're not,
I wish for you a lot,
I'm becoming something I'm not.

Call for me,
And I will come back
Never leave again.

I need to hear you say;
You love and missed me,
Too long I've been gone.

Hold on to me
Never let me go
And I will leave no more.

Lars Fonteyne (15)
Oslo International School, Norway

Post Mortem

'You took your hatred out on me, made a victim my head.
You never ever believed in me, I was your tourniquet.'

The steel shines upon her skin
As if it's reaching from within
Reflections vivid and cerise red
The pain is playing with her head

She's moving slowly, towards me
Though she finds it hard to breathe
I hear her crying in the dim
My heart feels guilty, glad within

I am afraid she will not die
But then I see it in her eyes
I crave with zest to have her dead
The sapphire, sour stare has now turned red

The blood is flowing through my veins
As I begin to feel the pain
My adored, abhorrent cheating wife
Made me heave out my lonely knife

The grotesque painting beside me
Shows the dimness of hell, dimness in me
The sacrilegious shadow revealed in the art
No love for Him, no love for her in my dying heart

They abandoned me, not the other way around
They do not deserve to live they're no more in me found
Like a griffin by a corpse, I wait beside her side
And watch the blood smoothly curl as I cry.

Boris Rudavskyy (15)
Oslo International School, Norway

I Will Come

(Inspired by Victor Hugo)

Through and over windswept plains
With buffeting horses' manes,
And on through deathly canyons
On mighty charging stallions.
Across the wild and stormy sea
To come to rest in your quiet lea.
To hear the last of your voice
I have no choice
But to come.

My eyes
Are streaming with unspoken goodbyes.
My heart
Is yearning for a brand new start.

I will come
To be by your side.

My heart is a streamlet of sorrow,
For no longer shall I see tomorrow.
But I will find the one who took your life
And he will have his own taste of strife.
And the light that once guided my heart
Is now tearing my soul apart,
For I left it
With the roses
By your grave.

Sean Hagerty (12)
Pinewood International School, Greece

What If The World Was Gone?

What if the world was gone?
We've been polluting it for so very long.
The world has become a little piece
Of glass inside a compressor.
What if the world was gone?
We'd all be like a bug under a foot.
What if the world was gone?
There'd be nothing.
We'd be thin air.
Just what if this were to happen?

Marco Bustamante (11)
Pinewood International School, Greece

A Poem, Some Music And A Tear

How can I write a poem
With no music
With no sound
With no voice to sing?

How can I write a poem
With no tears?
Tears which are in me
And give me in a poem.

My mind makes a poem
And my hand writes it.

A poem is music.
Music is a tear.
A tear is happy sadness.
And all this is love.

Arts of nothing and of everything.
Arts as meanings of life
And madness.

Emily Koufa (15)
Pinewood International School, Greece

Can't Hold Me Down

What has happened to the world?
Women have given up the fight - no more 'Can't hold me down.'
I'll buy myself a platinum blonde wig
And help girls with my award-winning grin.
'No life without a man' takes the place of 'Life without a man'.
Little girls *and* boys - seen, not heard.
I mean, how can a child have an opinion?

Girls sent through private schools, only to become housewives?
Is this ambition?
What has happened to *our* world?
They speak of change and human rights,
But we are far short of development.
So much for 'Children of the Future'.
Oh yeah, and getting low grades is cool.
Who wants a nerd?
Pressure on children, not to be unique, but all the same.
Attitude, smoking - and you're one of the gang.

What has happened to my world?
Wake up!
50% of the population is female, unbelievable I know!
So don't oppress us.

('Women are too stupid to work' is depressing enough -
without it coming from the mouth of a 11-year-old!)

Please, don't just laugh and tell me to cool it, or ease off.
I can't change who I am, I have to like it or lump it.
But I feel no desire to be cool - not if *this* is the modern definition.
What has happened to your world?
Call me a dork or a geek.
Let me see you try.
Because you certainly
Can't hold *me* down.

Natalia Kappos (13)
Pinewood International School, Greece

Thinking Of The Never Thought

One day,
One night,
Imagine.
Think.
Think of something that was never thought of
Open up a new world of dreams
Made by you
By your thoughts
Think of the ground, think of the grass
Think of cars, pollution of gas
Think of dreams
Dreams that can change it all
Dreams that control your thought
Make those dreams come true by thinking
Thinking of the poor, the ill, the hungry
Make their wish come true by your thought
Make them dream the dreams made by you
Fulfil their dreams
Help them also to think
Of the never thought.

Alex Shevtsov (12)
Pinewood International School, Greece

Ambition

Ambition is a fearsome enemy
Whose lonely, desperate nature
Cruelly seizes the human instinct
For a peaceful, harmonious life.
Creating a monstrous new race,
Astonishing and indescribable,
Whose life is brutally drained,
Causing them to be driven
By distorted desire and pride.
For an intangible power and control
Makes them clash with themselves
Causing the Devil's most diabolical face
To come alive on the surface of the Earth.
Out of this, where will we find
Permanent, unconditional peace
That will last to the end
And lead us into the beginning
Of the prologue
Of brightening darkness?

Antoine Jost (15)
Pinewood International School, Greece

The Dance Of The Brown Leaf

I had never set foot here, even though I felt something familiar,
A feeling that awoke in me when I was left here.
I was sitting by the icy, pitch-black shore of the half-frozen lake,
Watching the red sun which shot
Rays of bleeding light over the still, silent lands,
But gave out no heat to warm and waken the sleeping nature.

There was nothing moving,
Besides the withered leaves on a tree,
A tree that had long ago fallen to sleep
Under the chilly cloak of coming winter.

I sat there still, not wanting to think of what had happened
Over the past few months,
Not willing to accept the consequences of actions done,
Of words said.
Nothing mattered now,
Now that I had lost the sense of a warm feeling flowing out of me
Of the love I had once had for others.

I watched the dance of a brown leaf.
It followed the wind, until it led to the centre of the lake,
Where the leaf fell and floated on the glowing surface for some time.
Finally, it sank into the silent darkness.

This reminded me so much of what I had done to her,
Like the wind leading her to . . . the never-ending darkness.

Anastasia Stoyanova (14)
Pinewood International School, Greece

What If . . .

What if in this world there was only peace?
No war and no killing and we could all live in tranquillity.

If in the world we all accept people without thinking of their looks
Or where they're from, without being racist or prejudice.

What if everyone could just walk outside without worrying who else
was there?
Or if they would bother you?

What if everyone could accept each other without thinking something
Else when they turn their back just to trust each other?

What if there was no crime in order to make the whole world fear just
the thought of it?
What if we didn't have to walk with someone at night for safety
instead of company?

What if this world could lend a hand to the poor and misfortunate,
What would happen?
What if we could all just help each other?

What if . . .
That is something we could only dream.

Thomas Michaelides (13)
Pinewood International School, Greece

Life In A Dream

If only I could close my eyes
And never wake up.
I desire life in a dream
Where everything is pure and beautiful
As mountain pools,
The world of the elves
And hidden beauty,
Far, far away from reality.
I want to live there in my dream,
Where at night my wishes come true,
When the moonlight gently touches my skin,
And the whistle of the wind whispers in my ears -
'Come, come, come'
Calling me to escape from reality
And blend with the mystery of eternity.
There into the world of bliss,
Where there is no pain, no grief, no sorrow.
That's where I belong.
That's where I find the real me.
There . . . in my dream . . .
In a secret never to be shared.
In my world I can fly, I can reach the sky.
And 'impossible' doesn't exist,
Because it's my creation -
I control it!

Mariya Hristova (15)
Pinewood International School, Greece

Everlasting Blue

The death of a friend washed away all the life in her.
That everlasting blue in her eyes became white.
She would stare at me like a ghost.
Pleading to save the everlasting blue.

Her broken heart,
A never-ending hole of darkness,
Was what she was falling through.
Because this friend was like other.
Her wind, her muse.

She is now nothing but sadness,
Stuffed with unhappiness and sorrow
That everlasting blue that shown brightly in her eyes
Is gone.

I walked into her room, which was now lifeless
And saw her. I saw exactly what I expected.
Her limp body,
Her howling parents
Yet, the smile on her face.
The everlasting blue was awakened,
In her eyes.

She is there now, with her muse,
Happier than ever.
She would have been miserable if she hadn't ended this,
This heartbroken life she was living.
So I just walked away, not feeling any emotion
Because her soul was already lifeless, before her body was.
I took comfort in the fact knowing that
The everlasting blue,
Would stay . . . everlasting.

Celena Wasserstrom (13)
Pinewood International School, Greece

Imagination

Every person in the world
Can imagine
They imagine a world
Without war and borders
They imagine a world
In peace
They imagine a world
United
And they get ideas,
And hope
And some thoughts
And they improve
The world
With imagination

Imagination: what all people have
What all people live with
Is the key
To the land of dreams

Jaekyung Han (12)
Pinewood International School, Greece

My Whispering Storm

(Dedicated to the remaining Bengal Tigers of the world)

My storm speaks, but only a few care to hear,
He quietly listens, while all around others shout.
His world as he knows it is no longer!
Why . . . how, does he tolerate this intrusion?
And without a single windy hiss.
But I'll stand by him, my storm.
Next time my storm tries to speak, I'll hush the others.
His perfect blue tiger eyes will gleam,
And my storm's radiant, white coat will show his true royalty!
His sleek black stripes will stand out proudly,
But his whispering days are over!
Now the world shall hear his mighty roar, like thunder!
And all will acknowledge his presence, as they listen dumbfounded.
They will see, as I have seen all along,
And they too will hear and know.
That my storm is only a ferocious beast if you choose to see him
that way.
But like a storm, he too can be calming, and make things clear
after he passes.
Every storm is calm in its own eye.
My calm Bengal storm.
But if you listen to his roar, he will tell you of his plight,
His plea to all mankind.
We must all unite to save him, for he is in danger.
My dear Bengal storm.

Chanelle Zaphiropoulos (11)
St Catherine's British Embassy School, Greece

A Horse's Prayer

Master, a call for help,
Care for me and feed me well,
Use your voice,
And not the reins,
Don't squash my tongue with the bit.

Grant my wish,
And give me some,
Some love and freedom,
I don't ask a lot . . .

Please my master,
It's up to you,
Don't slay me with
Your hand and whip!

All I ask
Is a dream,
And if you grant
I will work
And if I work
I will please . . .

Amen.

Amaryllis Goulandris (11)
St Catherine's British Embassy School, Greece

Meaning Of Life

Life is to be kind and caring
That means that you should be sharing
Life can change from one moment to the other
So that's why we should listen to our mother!

Life has some bad things
Which can disturb you in your dreams
Life is not always easy
And sometimes it gets really busy

Life can also get exciting
And sometimes even frightening
Always try your best
But make sure you get some rest!

Don't forget life is fantastic
Even if you are sarcastic
Life is about love and hope
So do your best and try to cope!

Gina Dooley (12)
St Catherine's British Embassy School, Greece

Knowing You're Alive is The Meaning Of Life

I knew I was alive
When I heard my first tune
When I managed my first dive
When I got a new bedroom

I know I'm alive
Every time I dance
When I learn something new
And try to advance

I know I will be alive
Whatever may be
And I'll always remember
To just be me

Knowing you're alive is the meaning of life.

Margarita Fox (11)
St Catherine's British Embassy School, Greece

The Meaning Of Life

We're always asking what the meaning of life is,
For everyone it's a different thing,
So sit down awhile, to share my thoughts with you.
Life is being with family,
And having fun.
It's to never stop trying and getting things done,
And even when times are bad,
You have to fight and struggle, don't stay sad.
Life is education and discovering the world around us,
Learning to love each other and share our different points of view.
It's sometimes tough, sometimes an adventure.
Life is a mystery, full of surprises, dressed in all kinds of disguises!
It's rainbows and sunshine and ups and downs,
Enjoying every small moment that God has sent.
Things whiz by and we always ask why.
So let's say no to war, hunger and poverty,
Try to live in peace and harmony.
Remember to smile, it's not about having it all.
It's about achieving and believing and having a ball!
We only get one chance to find where we belong in this world,
So let's make a difference.

Vicki Kassioula (12)
St Catherine's British Embassy School, Greece

The Meaning Of Life

The meaning of life is to have lots of fun
To jump into water and lay in the sun
To take our first steps
And to go to school
Say our first word
To enter the world

But it's not just about fun
We have hard times too
We should be sad from time to time
But then . . .
That's what friends are for
To help us and cheer us up

We should earn what we want
Go to school and then onto college
Then we work and lead our own life
And that's the meaning of life!

Alex Capras (11)
St Catherine's British Embassy School, Greece

Darkened Alley

Walking down a darkened alley,
Children playing in their backyard,
Wind is blowing, leaves are flowing down toward you ever more.

Suddenly a man walks by and all the movement is firm and still,
I could cut the tension with a knife,
But the man keeps walking evermore.

I am nearly at the end,
Cars are flashing by and by,
I am nearly at the end of my journey,
But leaves and men keep going evermore.

Theo Haines (14)
St George's British International School, Italy

Tricolour

Woke up this morning
But the green from our flag
Was found to be dead

I thought I was dreaming
But the fields and the mountains
Turned out to be black

Next it was white's turn,
Clouds from the sky
Dropped to earth, to die

I thought I was dreaming
But the swans and daisies
Turned out to be black

You would not expect it,
But they did keep the red
Bloodstains on your freedom
It just had to be shed

The land of our fathers
A cage for our sons
Is this all that we're here for
Is it maybe for God?

Ludovico Tallarita (16)
St George's British International School, Italy

Sorrow

The pain who sleeps at night,
The waves who crash on the hard strong rocks,
The sun so strong that tans you, but
The fire will burn you,
The salty sea will cure you,
The vortice will kill you,
But you can survive,
One day the rain will fall and wash your pain away,
Like the salt of the sea after the burn on the skin from the fire.

Caterina Chhabra (17)
St George's British International School, Italy

Lily Pad

I once looked through a telescope
And saw glimpse of place
A place so big, I felt unsafe.

I once swam in the ocean
I could not sense nor see the bottom
A place so big, I felt unsafe.

I once fell from the sky
A never-ending distance
An unpredictable speed
A place so free I felt unsafe.

I once sat on a lily pad
Along with fellow Salientia
A priceless moment to cherish
A place so simple I felt safe.

Celestina Ren (17)
St George's British International School, Italy

Like, Like, Like

Words like have a way of being repeated,
Like words repeated like without being noticed.
Words repeated like when said,
But like not noticed when read.
It's like all inside us, like a ball of words
Throwing out like only the same words every time.
Like words repeated like unconsciously
When like speaking and like thinking.
Words like cloned like too many times,
Are like taking over like our life
Without like being able to shake them out,
Like until we like accept these words as like normal.
And now above this line there are twenty words named like.
And now there's twenty-one.

Andrea Calla (14)
St George's British International School, Italy

Another Day

Another day in that dark, dull place,
Where air is fusty,
People walking up and down,
In every direction.

Some waiting impatiently,
Others quietly,
Waiting for arrival,
Running out of time.

A rush of air,
Lights coming out from the darkness,
People grabbing their bags,
Standing up and watching.

Thousands of reflections,
People come out, others go in,
Locked inside, they fade away,
Off to their destination,
Just another day in the metro station.

Isabelle Zonderland (17)
St George's British International School, Italy

Eccedentesiast

She walked past the hall smiling in a fake way, a face that tries to trick
everyone with that same expression
Whether she is happy or sad it's always identical.
People always stare at her whilst she is being fake,
All she wants is friends,
But that's not the way.
People don't understand why she can't just be herself.
The laugh, the look on her face tricks some people, but not others.
I ask myself, 'Why is she like this?'

Emily Marranci (14)
St George's British International School, Italy

The Stranger

He walked into town
With his hat low on his face
He made not a sound
As he moved at a slow pace.

With his back to the sun
Nothing need be said
For their work left undone
Villagers gazed at him instead.

He stopped in the main street
And said with a gentle voice
'I will, as a special treat,
Grant one wish of your choice.'

The villagers all got in a rush
People of all ages shouted out
'I want a boat' 'I want a brush'
Everything they could think about.

As the neighbours fought
The foreigner sighed
He knew he was caught
This is how it went every time.

'Let's wish to be happy'
One little boy finally cried.
The crowd started clapping
And the stranger openly sighed.

The villagers all went to bed
Comforted that the next day
Just like the stranger said
They would be happy.

At sunrise, the stranger left
The townspeople tried to
Call to him to come back
There was nothing they could do.

They wanted to explain
But they could only gasp like a fish
And the man kept walking down the lane
Ignoring their hopes for one more wish.

The man had decided
After all he had heard that it was their words
That made them unhappy.
To keep his promise, he walked away with their words.

Lauren Berdick (13)
St George's British International School, Italy

Fame

Mondialisation, globalisation
Globalizacion all mean the same.
People are moving around
The world for fame.

People are leaving their
Native places, with their wives.
They do it just to get
Some extraordinary pace in their lives.

Everyone is choosing to
Travel for fun.
While doing this they
Dislike rain and want sun.

We find lots of police
In airports for security.
But there are many
Tourists in seaports with liberty.

Agencies are making lots of money
When couples publicise their love.
This happens often when it's sunny
But you still find people giving a shove.

Viplava Jain (14)
St George's British International School, Italy

Sense Of Myself?

I wake up every morning,
In the same warm and cosy bed,
I always have the same view,
From my sleepy head.

I eat the same things for breakfast,
The same old basic food,
Nothing new for me to report,
In my bored and dreary mood.

I take the exact same journey,
In the same old big blue car,
Seeing the same locations,
Nothing seems too afar.

Then when I get into school
There are the same faces there,
The same voices greeting me,
Nothing to make you stare.

I wear the same matching clothes,
Like most of everyone else,
This is an easy way of losing,
A true sense of yourself.

So when you look at my life,
Take a stepped-back point of view,
You wouldn't notice a thing,
Nothing you could report new.

Yes it may not seem too bad,
As I sit in my cosy flat,
Nothing I can complain about,
At least from where you're sat.

So these are my current borders,
That's what is restricting me,
A long yearning desire,
To know who I can be.

Katy Barber (15)
St George's British International School, Italy

Ms Prucher

Boys and girls this is your assignment
Look towards the top where you can find an equation
It's all written on the sheet I have given you
Questions, confusion.
Answers, frustration.
Equation! Equation! Enter your equation!
Look at what yours says: $Y = x + 2$

Boys and girls once you've finally gotten your equation
They do it for you, don't worry about trying it out for yourself.
Press, press, press
Try and try.

You've tried, but try and understand what 'we' are doing
They have written it for you
Just do what you are told.
You are always meant to do what you are told.
We are making it easier for you
Try and try
Confusion, questions?

Boys and girls, now we can label the graph
Everything has a label, a name, a heading
Make sure not to forget any line
You understand now?
Now you can continue, do the next step
(University, job, marriage, death)
Think for yourself
Don't ask questions.

Mahira Sobral (16)
St George's British International School, Italy

Words Are Overrated

One look, one glance, one touch to the skin
One wink, one smile, caresses me within

One sigh, one tear, tells me what you think
But when you talk, in uncertainty I sink

Two hands entwined, tell the world a story
Four eyes, shining bright, show off their glory

One quiet chuckle, seems to suffice
But longwinded explanations, fail to be concise

One shiver, one frown, alert me without fail
One honest expression, explains in detail

Two feet, one body, explains the dancing beat
But cloaked by music, words cease to be concrete

So when words are forgotten, writing begins to fade
I say, away with words, forget the masquerade
So close your mouth and set your feelings free
Since it's not your words but what you mean that moves me.

Alexander Snijders (16)
St George's British International School, Italy

Er Mortadella

He's a man that has ruined a country,
He's a man that has let everyone down,
He's a man with no dignity nor compassion,
He's a man that has gained the hate of every single person
In this country,
We live in a country of glory and fame and this man has embarrassed
Us in the whole world,
This man has destroyed our wall of fame and trust,
This man is a disaster,
And I speak in the name of all the people.

Nicola Di Napoli (14)
St George's British International School, Italy

My Dream

I dream that my dreams shall be more than just dreams.
I dream of making them a reality one day.
In my dreams I dream of peace.

I know my dreams will soon come true.

I dream to escape
The harsh reality of life.
The cold cruel world
That surrounds my life.
The poverty that destroys peace and creates war and war that brings
Death.

But I dream because
It keeps me safe
Just to know that my dream
Is the only place where I'm completely safe.

Bongani Malewa (16)
St George's British International School, Italy

Blown Away With Words

Blow away the words that hurt,
The words that make you sad.
Blow away all words that sting,
Those words are very bad.

Come to me with words so bright,
The words that sound so nice.
Come to me with all the words
Which make a person smile.

Blow me away with 'mind-blowing' words,
That make my dreams come true.
Mark my word, when words ring true,
They shine like diamonds for me and you.

Shamini Mathur (14)
St George's British International School, Italy

Star-Crossed Lovers

(Little summary of their story, an Israeli man and Jewish woman who are forbidden to live together, due to their religions, even though they are married. 'Elle, Magazine, September 2006')

A harmonious Tchaikovsky crescendo.

Blossomed, beamed and became
Roses blooming from buds
Daisies maturing from seeds
Streams thickening into rivers.
Pocahontas and her prince
Happily ever after
But alas! 'tis not this our story . . .

Two households, both alike in dignity!
Like Romeo and Juliet, in ancient Verona
Or the ordained Babylonian lovers
Pyramus and Thysbe.
By forces greater than themselves.
Across the borders of Jerusalem and Palestine,
Jasmine cannot bring her husband
To live off their love.

A love so astounding, a love so bright
Like a sinuously gracious plea
To the historical dove
That keeps failing to deliver
Its olive branch
To entwine the strands of religion,
Like a bridge of ropes
Across the concrete border.

Nothing can be done,
Nothing can be said,
The ministry has declared
'When there's a law, we must obey it.'

These star-crossed lovers continue
To pray, that everything will be alright
For a love so profound, so meek and so mild
Should not have to end.

Feuds so imprudent
So ruthless and so vile
Do represent a wall
So futile and so vain.
Through the chinks of the wall,
Jasmin and Osama
Poor souls,
Content to whisper.

A harmonious Tchaikovsky diminuendo.

Thakane Mafura (15)
St George's British International School, Italy

White Suits

(A poem about censorship and propaganda)

Guns fire out across the open plain,
Barbed wire and trenches.
A boy soldier, his life fading,
Lies bleeding in the dust.

And for what?
A canister of oil, another civil war,
While men in their white suits,
Talk of dictators.

Anarchy and poverty
Unspeakable together.
Politics and pain,
A handshake for the papers.

A lover, staring at the door,
Thinks of nights long gone.
Weeps at what might have been,
Another victim of endless war.

And for what?
A canister of oil, another civil war,
While men in their white suits,
Talk of dictators.

Fergus Johnson (13)
St George's British International School, Italy

Away With Words

We start with a man.
Now this not so ordinary man,
Is known as the 'charmed one'
He is S
S is strong, kind and good-looking.
The only problem he has, is that he can't talk to the ladies.

S works at the Royal Flash Shoe Company,
Where they promise pain, long working hours and no holidays.
S hates his work but he can't quit because there is no other job he
can do.
He normally comes home very late and is expected to be back at
work at 6am.

S has a friend called M
M is lazy, ugly and ungrateful (but not towards his friends)
M is a hawker and sells very cheap things like broken mobile phones.
M still likes his job.
M has two other friends called E and L.
E is kind, a bit lazy and helpful while L is just like S.
E and L are brothers, they work as waiters at the Mon Chèr Restaurant.
E and L get good payment and enough holidays.
They are quite lucky.

E and L have other friends called I and I
I and I come from Little I Street where everyone is rich.
The first I is a bit fat, sometimes crazy but loyal while the other I
Is intelligent and good looking.
I and I are twins but they don't do the same jobs:
One of them is a sales assistant while the other is a doctor.

One day all these friends went out for lunch.
They drank much beer and had an argument about who was going to
Have that last piece of pork chop.
All of a sudden a magical fairy came and somehow joined them up.
'Aaaaah!' screeched everyone.
The fairy said, 'Since you are all joined up you shall be called *simile.*'
The boys thought it was a pretty good name, and said so.

From that day they became friends again.
And till now the word simile has created other words eg. like, as, and
Many more.
Thanks to S, I, M, I, L and E.

Andre Maina (15)
St George's British International School, Italy

Away With Words

Cinnamon, cinnamon, cinnamon,
This is how I am called
I am the king of the spices.
I am very slender,
Practically a stick
I come from the inner bark of a cinnamon tree
My name is Cinnamon.

I look weak,
But strong in taste,
My flavour adds aroma to food
I am an unavoidable person,
In the Indian cuisine

I am precious and expensive
I am gifted to people,
Even though I am unattractive.
My oil is used for therapy,
To soothe tired skin.

Cinnamon, cinnamon, cinnamon
Oh now I'm being called to be powdered,
And then shaken into a drink,
I am just too cool,
To be a cinnamon!

Tarun Jacob (13)
St George's British International School, Italy

Your Heart Song

Read between the lines, for there lies a hidden meaning
A meaning you can only think you know
The words mask the truth like a veil covers the face
See the emotions in your body take life
Emotions and feelings triggered by simple words
These words take you on a journey
A journey through the depths of your mind
Where you have no boundaries, no limits, you can touch the sky
The power a song holds is like no other
A song can touch you so deeply, move you in a way only you
                                        can see

There's a mark it leaves like a loveheart carved in a tree
It can bring back a smile when you cry
Or it can bring a tear to the eye
The song has a way with words so
Let the chorus carry you
Let the verse veer you
Let the words have their way with you.
You'll know when they're done
'Cause forever you will have a song in your heart
A song that will never part
Only you can write the lyrics to your life song
Only you can decide when the song will end.

Mia Ruffo (14)
St George's British International School, Italy

Taste The Silence

Hear him rustle
Hear him howl
Hear him move
And hear him prowl;

See his shadow
Soaring low
See his eyes,
See their glow;

Smell the pine trees
Smell the night
Smell the essence
Of moonlight;

Feel his claws
Digging deep
Feel the pain
Feel it creep;

Taste the silence
Taste the death . . .
It steals your courage,
Steals your breath;

Speak of wisdom,
Speak bitter sounds
Too cold and distant
To melt on the ground . . .

Marianna Vincenti (13)
St George's British International School, Italy

Fallen Lighthouse

The seas and the skies,
Were combined together in one.
The wind rustled,
Moving and touching the water.
The water embracing the wind.
Ripples forming,
It meant only one thing;
Rain.
The water rose higher,
Forming waves bigger than skyscrapers.

On the other side on a headland,
There was what,
A lighthouse probably.
With its light shining brighter than stars,
In the night lack, like the colour
Of coal. The wind,
Now pushed the waves
Making them humongous and gigantic.
With the force of a whole stampede
Of elephants.
Stronger than the horns of the
Toughest ram it battered and battered.
The lighthouse.
With the last breath, the lighthouse
Tumbled and tumbled.
With the wind's rage,
The bricks dropped one by one,
Plop, plop, plop into the sea.

The sea calmed down, the clouds departed
Throwing the sunshine. You could hear
The waves whisper dead, down, ruined at last.

Davide Baldanzi (13)
St George's British International School, Italy

A First Word

Two little bundles of warmth clutching at its mother's neck
The beating of a young heart,
A quick playful rhythm
And the soft pink flesh
Of a child
Rubbing against the woman's cheek
A tiny pair of pastel pink lips feeling
Its way around its mother
And then
Comes the word.
'Mamma,' the child sings
'Mamma'
A heavy thump of the woman's heart,
A boom of exploding excitement
Touching, moving, beautiful lullaby to a mother
A silent smile of tenderness to her lips,
But no words
She wants to hear her child say it again, and
Again
The child's voice, the word, the sounds of
An expression of love for its mother
Echoing in her ears
The banging on the table
The hysterical laughter it makes
And the pinching of material on the couch, between little fingers
All the while gurgling
'Mamma'
Everything is
'Mamma'
But secretly
She knows it's for her,
Only her
His first word,
For only her.

Allisa Kouki (14)
St George's British International School, Italy

B-Ball

Some people consider this game lame
But to me it's a bit more than a game
From where I'm from, ain't only about going for the jumpers
It's also tryin' 'em fancy crossovers
For more than a century B-ball has been ruling the street
It's been great for people who've got issues using their feet
Being able to take it down for a slam
Although it ain't always gonna be an easy jam.

B-ball is a game full of passion
If ya'll know what I'm talking about
Guaranteed for those who are down with action
Although I would say I hate it when they shout
Always on about hope and determination
And for those who got dilemmas finding a sport - B-ball is the sport
for you.

Ed Dane Medi (15)
St George's British International School, Italy

Where Are You From?

Some people live in many different places during their life
They taste different cultures
They learn different styles of living
They get to know new traditions, and so on . . .
Is this a positive thing or a negative thing?
The fact that when you're asked 'Where are you from?'
You don't have an answer . . .
But on the other hand when you're asked:
'How many languages do you speak?'
You can answer five . . .
Is it better to create your life in one single place
Or to create your life in different places?

Edolo Ghirelli (14)
St George's British International School, Italy

Avocado

A mixture of textures
In one pear-shaped fruit,
A dark, wrinkly outer shell
Hiding the softness inside.
Slice, a knife glides through the fruit,
Stop.
The knife hits the impenetrable stone concealed inside,
The heart of this mysterious fruit.
Dark green lustre,
Inside sunny yellow
Or maybe luminous green?
It depends.
Sweet or sour?
A distinct taste, this fruit has.
It's not a pear nor a mango,
It's not like any fruit.
It's not a dessert,
A salad? To eat with a meal?
You decide.
It's an avocado.

Mikaela Patrick (15)
St George's British International School, Italy

Anna-Molly (Anomaly)

I watch the ships pass by and I wonder, where she might be,
Anna-Molly, anomaly, Anna-Molly,
She always deviates from what is normal or accepted,
Anna-Molly, anomaly, Anna-Molly,
You never know what she is going to do next,
Anna-Molly, anomaly, Anna-Molly,
She is different but nevertheless beautiful,
Anna-Molly, anomaly, Anna-Molly,
Just when you think you figured her out . . . she disappears,
Anna-Molly, anomaly, Anna-Molly.

Esteban Altamirano (15)
St George's British International School, Italy

Words Can Hurt

When I first heard those words,
I trembled inside, wondering
'Is it true? Is it really over?'
Never considered I would hear those words.

Thought I was invincible,
Too strong to fall,
But obviously I got knocked down
By words that can hurt.

Seeing those objectionable words
Come out of your mouth,
Like a venomous snake gliding out of its basket,
Devastated me, my heart, devastated my mind.

And now, I puzzle over questions,
From which I will never get answers,
Reflect on simple words with lots of meaning,
Who's response would harm me even more.

But you know how I feel,
You know you hurt me, but don't care.
And thinking of it, they were just words,
Just simple, deathly words that can hurt.

Ludovica Di Canio (14)
St George's British International School, Italy

When I Am In Nature

When I am in the nature
When I am in the wild
I am in my world.
My world where I can find whatever I want
A paradise with nobody commanding me
But nature.

Alberto di Giovanni (14)
St George's British International School, Italy

Words, Words, Words

Words, words, words where do I begin?
There are all kinds of words in the English language.
But what do they mean? Words don't explain anything!
They are just groups of letters assigned together.
There are very long words like 'Antidisestablishmentarianism',
But to me they are merely a load of mumble-jumble!
My first words were not that great and definitely not educational,
Unless you think that 'Oh no!' was a good use of language.
Summ ppl tlk like this, while others use 'Old language',
But what does this all mean? Nothing! Annoying but true!
I could say, tyrannosaurus rex when it is simpler to say T-rex,
So you kids at home don't listen to how to 'languaginize' yourself,
When you can lie back at home and make your own language!

Kieran Wilkie (14)
St George's British International School, Italy

Speechless

He was mute,
But only his voice didn't sound.
In the deep pits of purgatory,
On the walls his fists pound.

He screamed on the inside,
He recalled what she said,
And how he had chosen,
The lies he was fed.

A condemned man walked by,
A kind look on his face.
A flicker of light in the dark,
But then it was gone, with agony in its place.

He stands there alone,
With no one to share,
His speechless, non-life.
Instead of silent, screams of despair.

Julia Galway-Witham (14)
St George's British International School, Italy

A New Start

Prodi
Bush
Blair
Bin Laden
Putin
These are only some of the names
That have been camping in my head
For a long time now
All I hear is politics
All I hear is war
All I hear is death
All I hear is hungry children
I want to stop hearing
All I see is blood
All I see are weapons
All I see are corpses
I want to stop seeing
I have to clear my brain
Too many words are pressing against the side of my head
I'm going to start all over again
The first word
That enters my brain
Peace
The second
Love
And the third
Free
Let's try and live a better life
Without war
Death
Blood
But with
Peace
Love
And freedom.

Stefano Spalvieri (15)
St George's British International School, Italy

The Cycle Of Words

Silence
Birth, no words
A breath, a cry,
Two tears
No words.

Childhood,
Adolescence,
Adulthood.

First step,
First word,
First freedom,
First love,
First sex,
First hope,
First pain,
First truth,
First lies,
First questions,
First fears.

Just words,
Two tears,
Last cry, last breath,
Death
Silence.

Jessica Moens (15)
St George's British International School, Italy

Lost In The Darkness

I am lost. Lost in the deep thoughts
I am lost in a jigsaw puzzle that I cannot solve
My legs are trembling, struggling to move
The still sound
The echoing footsteps coming closer
My mind is in a maze field that I cannot come out of
Will I survive all this trouble in the darkness?
My heart starts beating faster and faster
Anticipating the dark figure moving closer and closer
I am lost in words puzzled by the events happening
The object is very close but I cannot visualise it
My heart feels of emptiness
Everything goes suddenly
My dream is lost. Lost forever
That I cannot remember.

David Luma (16)
St George's British International School, Italy

Eight

Eight, the number I sometimes hate,
Its utterance is sometimes like someone
Scratching their fingernails across a blackboard.
Eight times I have been left by the bus,
Eight times per week I have to do chores,
Eight times I have lost my ID.

It's eight and I am late for a game
Which would decide my fate.
Games like these grow on you with
Ease and are hard to let go,
Like a kitten playing with a ball of yarn.

Eight, the number I get after rolling the dice,
After telling my life my final goodbye.
Eight, the number of times I have won at this game,
But I have a feeling it is all about to change.

Timothy Maina (17)
St George's British International School, Italy

Orange

I once caught the sun
It was a deep yellow tinged with red
I caught it as it was about to peep behind the hills.
And laid it in my hands
It rolled to and fro
Its tough shell
Like skin I know so well.

A shield/barrier/defence
For the jewel within
Flowing always in one direction
Tapering to one point.
To finish off the masterpiece
They award a medal
A green star like a brooch completing and complementing
The piece.

Searching I see no entrance
No joints or creases
As to enter, my way is blocked
Puzzled nails scrabble
To no avail
Just then the walls fall under a clean stroke
The acidic spray
Like pus from a wound
Tearing the shell apart
There is not one but many
I see 12 crescent moons
Fitting like some puzzle inconceivable to us now
Thin membranes spiderweb across
Sweet and juicy
Sharp and soft
Name and colour
Synonymous.

Aaron Matthew (15)
St George's British International School, Italy

Ode To Everything On My Desk Including The Pen Used To Write This Poem

English notebook,
You are a blue
Of navy sea inspired hues
Made out of murdered trees,
Compressed and dyed, written inside
Almost every other day. You sacrifice your lifespan
(Which is quite long, considering your insulting lack of
(bio-degradability)
To save me from my blissful ignorance and
Engulf me in priceless knowledge
Which helps me express my admiration towards your
Billions of lined capacities
And
Perforated
Paper
Sides.

And iPod, how shall I express my gratitude to the endless raucous
Contributions
You have so violently bestowed on my agonising eardrums by
Sending electric impulses across the spindly wires of headphones?
Only by saying that I wish you were not so prone to death, not so
Dependant for your own sake,
On my constant care,
On my iPod charger.

And you!
My box of matches,
My beloved,
My betrothed,
My pyromaniac instigator,
Your magic spark releases a strong smell of sulphur
And a delicate trickle of
Starry smoke
That swivels into the air
Like a current that ignores the laws of gravity.

You are responsible for lighting the tips of my
Blonde hair on fire,
That one time that I used your offspring to bring life
To a candlewick
And leaned carelessly over your newborn baby,
(That feeble flicker of a flame!)
Feeding thermal energy to the fibrous strands that cascaded
Towards the ground as shrivelled,
Curled,
Ashen . . .
Rather than split golden strings
Protruding from my scalp.

But unforgettable,
Undeniable
Is the credit owed to this pen,
This pen which writes my thoughts
In symbols and squiggles
That only people belonging to certain literate
Cultures
Will be blessed to read,
Privileged to waste a few minutes
Of the time
That they will
Never gain back on.

Cecilia Granara (15)
St George's British International School, Italy

One Last Shot

She smiled ever so gently as the sun shone upon her face.
It was the last day of the last month.
Could it be that this would be the last time I had a shot at my dream?
I felt hesitant,
I felt the adrenaline rushing through my body,
I was scared that this was the last shot,
Last time I saw my narrow dream.
I took a deep breath
And quietly said to myself, 'You can do it, make it through
and just try one last time.'
In a flash I started to reminisce about a vivid place
in the back of my mind
Where everything was perfect and I didn't have to worry about anything.
'Pull together,' I said, 'it's just an imaginary thought.'
I walked across the room as quiet as I could,
Blocking everything out from reality,
I'll give it my all and give it my last shot . . .

Taonga Luma (14)
St George's British International School, Italy

Bomb

I was lying on the surface of the world,
When a bomb struck me,
A mixture of happiness and sadness,
The difference between life and death.

Life is like a bird,
It flies away easily,
Into a new reality,
Which one day we will discover.

So when that bird dies,
Like a bomb struck
All blows around you
And that is life!

Gaig Tonucci (15)
St George's British International School, Italy

He Is The One . . .

He is the one that gives me strength
He is the one that gives me courage
He is someone who I trust
He is the one that picks me up when I'm down
But now everything has changed . . .
He has cancer, it is incurable . . .
The doctor said he has one month of life
The final run has come
He doesn't know about his illness
We keep it secret so that he can live happily
He hides his pain when I'm near him
He is my best friend . . . there will always be a space
In my heart for you . . . thanks Grandpa Toni.

Luca Paganini (13)
St George's British International School, Italy

Timmerman The Dog

At home I've a precious cocker
Who's not a magnificent rocker,
He is black and white
But he doesn't bite
And he's really no good at soccer.

He is extremely cute,
You cannot call him a brute,
He drops his hairs
All over the stairs
But in fact he's very astute.

This dog is not very fat,
In Belgium he was chased by a cat!
You'll probably say, 'Boo'
But it's actually true,
And no one is as silly as that!

Anna Harvey-Kelly (11)
Scuola Europea di Varese, Italy

Visiting The Beach

The sky and sea are blue
The beach balls and bikinis are too!
There's multicoloured towels
And sunburnt girls with scowls
There are ten buckets just over there
And holes in the sand just everywhere.
I tell you
The sky is really blue
And you can have a barbecue.

Now the beach is deserted
Because the winter has come
No seagulls in the sky
And you can also spy
On people walking by.
They think there's no one there
But here's me sitting on a chair!

Rea Djaratou Steinberger (10)
Scuola Europea di Varese, Italy

A Potion

Eye of rat
Lung of bat
Black balloon
Skin of baboon
Scale of dragon
Tooth of wolf
Tongue of whale
Blood of male
Last of all
Mix it all
And rub
On throat
And be a goat!

Anna Isabella Manghi (10)
Scuola Europea di Varese, Italy

Jenny My Love

Jenny my love
Jenny my everything
I love you so much
And as well care for you.

Jenny my love
Jenny my everything
Your sweet pink nose
Is as soft as can be.

Jenny my love
Jenny my everything
Over the jump
You fly like a star.

Jenny my love
Jenny my everything
You are in my mind
Day after day
A sweet grey pony
As cute as can be
Forever and ever
Is waiting for me.

Sofie Christiansen (11)
Scuola Europea di Varese, Italy

Summer Trip

'Boiling, what a sweaty tum,
My pants are sticking to my bum.
Can't we stop for a moment or two?
I've got a rock in my shoe.

I'm soaked in sweat,'
'Shut up, don't fret!'
'It's so hot I want to scream
But at last I see an ice cream!'

Erica Geneletti (10)
Scuola Europea di Varese, Italy

Time's Running Out

The ice caps are melting
The seas are warming
The message is clear
We've had our warning
If you don't do something
Before too long
The world as we know it will be long gone.

Imogen Eddings (10)
Scuola Europea di Varese, Italy

Winter

Winter flew
Through the empty field.
Freezing grain and crops.
Tore each plant and buried each seed,
And then flew on.

Winter crept
Through cosy campsites.
Cooling each campfire
Swayed each branch and leaf,
But never a good thing, he gave.

Winter spun
Around empty cities.
Dropping every dead leaf
Shaking glass windows and doors
But still danced on.

Winter spiralled
Around a grumbling school,
Chilling children and teachers.
Ice is melting and so is winter
And fading away into spring.

Paloma Rao (11)
Sunny View School, Spain

Walking In Mr Walker's Shoes

My first thought in the morning -
Oh, not another day of school!
And those students think that being made
To learn the facts is cruel!
Try teaching them to a school of goldfish
In one ear and out the other,
No point at all to this job I have . . .
Why do I even bother?

Diego, get out!
Isabel, sit down!
There's always a reason to wear a frown.
Listen to them screeching out,
'Mr Walker, I don't get it!'
'Mr Walker, I forgot my brain!'
What d'you want me to do about it?
If you want to ask them out,
Then don't do it in my lesson!
Outrageous, when this school day ends
It'll be a blessing.
Making fun of my sunhat,
And because I have no hair . . .
Life would be so much easier if
9A wasn't there!

Reading pointless poems about mermaids
While all my friends are out to lunch.
I want to join but I'm stuck here
There's no hope for this brainless bunch!
Was that the bell? Oh finally!
Now all my teaching stress and sorrow
Is bottled up, impatient to be
Released again tomorrow.

Ishani Rao (14)
Sunny View School, Spain

Winter

Winter arrived
From the freezing North
To the warm South.
His wind rushed and tore the leaves off
His rain refused to stop and converted land into lake.

Winter whipped
The trees and buildings
And the sea became furious.
Then the snow came with her white cape
And dressed the woods as a bride.

Winter came,
And froze the falling water in the cascade.
Then the days became cold
While rain and wind rushed
But winter had already been told.

Winter made,
The storm fall much harder
And encouraged the wind to blow and blow.
They were becoming weaker
So they asked him to stop. Winter said, 'No!'

Winter left
With the clouds behind him
While the sun rose.
Winter was beaten
He was frightened from head to toe.

Claudia Jimenez (11)
Sunny View School, Spain

Reminiscence

I stand at the garden's old rusty gate
Its rough edges graze my fingers
I peek through the cursive bars at the orchard's fate
And my thought lingers.

Tight ropes of weeds scar the ground
Growing, clutching, cutting
The frail skin of the withered land.

A breeze of wind haunts the desolate scene
Howling, wailing, crying
It mourns the place serene
Quietly dying.

Dark, dreary clouds drape the sky.
Dripping, dribbling tears
Soak the wallowing ground.

A glimpse of black-grey wings
A crow glides from the shadows
In the darkness it sings
At the garden's oak tree gallows.

The garden's haunted entrance
Brings bits of a memory, remembrance
Of blooming springs
Which to the orchard clings.

Camilla Montonen (15)
The English School, Finland

Runaway

I run away from you at the mist of the morning.
I clear my way out of the dim forest.
Bitterly I scurry over the valleys.
Furiously I push through the dark waters,
Away, far away from you.

I feel the tears of despair blind my eyes.
I feel your frozen hand hunting my heart,
Disabling my mind.
I can feel you pulling, ripping, tearing me.
And knowing that I am too weak, my love,
I surrender with agony.
Bruising my beliefs and wishes,
You laugh and hug me,
Whispering that I'm yours forever.

I crawl still away from you.
With my faith,
With my bloody nails,
I try to drag myself,
Away, far away from you.

But my love, darkness, master,
You know.
You know that you are there.
Eternally.
Here.
In my heart.

Fida Kettunen (16)
The English School, Finland

Life And Death

You open your eyes and face the light,
A raindrop falls on your forehead,
You timidly begin to glide,
Along the smooth valley through the night,
Until the shady path brings a dark forest in sight.

You wish to advance but hesitate,
A second raindrop falls on your cheek,
In front of you, a forest black, a forest bleak,
A hostile labyrinth lies right ahead.
You flinch from fear, but go on instead,
You plough through mud, you wade through trees,
You face a door, you've got no keys,
You seem to find another way,
You're lost and start to run away.
You struggle, stumble, sometimes fall.
Yet you don't quit; you even crawl.
But after hopeless tries that come,
You finally yield and you succumb.

And then the white light reappears,
Long after wrecked and desperate years,
Putting an end to all your fears,
Illuminating the exit
You're so exhausted, you cannot respond,
You just let go and let yourself be carried beyond.
A third and last raindrop lands on your lips,
You take a final taste and move towards the exit.

Maria Christophi (16)
The Grammar School, Cyprus

Him

As she cries to her tear-stained pillow again,
She is captivated by feelings of wonder, worry and isolation . . .
All because of him . . .

She remembers the day she first saw him,
When she became mesmerised,
In a stranger's eyes.

After the awkward introduction they became 'good' friends.
But her grades were slipping; her friends were becoming non-
existent,
Her family worried
All because of the time spent with him.

She truly had lost control.
As he had captivated her soul.
And technically destroyed her as a whole.
As she became dangerously lost in him . . .

The beginning of the end came with one rainy and stormy night,
When they were alone together.
He swept her off her feet with an abrupt kiss overwhelming her
with happiness,
Yet it didn't stop with the kiss.
He did what he came to do whilst ignoring her sobs and pleas.
Her heartbreaking cries of denial pierced the silence of the night.
But he wouldn't stop . . .

That night, two months later,
Still lurked in the depths of her memory forever to remain there.
As in her heart there is now a hole,
And guess what else,
In her stomach there is also a new soul.

She thought he had everything.
Thought he was perfect for her.
Yet it turned out that all he ever had,
Was the ability to scar a person for life,
As he ran away with his words . . .

Roberta Raftopoulos (16)
The Grammar School, Cyprus

The Lovely Lake

It
Followed

It wasn't far away
Instead we went to a lake
We thought it was a story
And everything was fake

Green everywhere
And also blue
We really loved it
We couldn't move!

It was a dream
There was a white dove
Flying everywhere
Like spreading love

No one there
Only us
How cool
No one to fuss

It went eight
It was night
We had to go back
Before there was no light!

Nicoletta Tsanou (12)
The Grammar School, Cyprus

B-Ball For All

It's time to bounce
And I mean to bounce
To make the ball pounce
So let me announce

B-ball for all B-ball for all
I like to bounce da ball
Especially in da mall
Where it's nice and big B-ball for all.

I like to lay-up
It keeps da game up
To brighten da day up
So get ready to bounce, uh-huh, yeah, wozzup

I like to shoot
Da ball through dat hoop
It runs through like soup.
There's the three point, the free throw, and the alley 001.

Then there's the dunk
It's a kind of funk
It's difficult junk
Unless you're a B-ball punk.

B-ball for all, B-ball for all
I hope you learn da basics of how to play B-ball.

George Christoforou (11)
The Grammar School, Cyprus

Ice Cream

Ice cream is cold like winter,
It is icy like snow.
Ice cream is colourful
And it reminds me of the rainbow
Ice cream is perfect and I
Love it!

Fani Lophitou (12)
The Grammar School, Cyprus

What Can I See?

Everybody listen!
I want to speak!
Why don't you care
About me?

It's the first time
I don't want to hear you.
I just want to fly
Into your thoughts.

Look through someone else's eyes.
What can you see?
I better tell you first
What I can see.

Stand in front of me.
Open your eyes.
Open your world
And let me in.

I can see the sky of dreams,
The stars of hopes,
The clouds of love
And the sun of smiles.

I can see a better world
Where everyone is happy.
I can see the ocean of life
And all this through your eyes!

So, please don't close your eyes.
Let them open and don't say a word.
Just let the sun from your eyes
Shine onto our world!

Frantzeska Lambidoniti (13)
The Grammar School, Cyprus

The Wildest Animal, Human!

Too many wars are happening
And thousands of victims suffering

I see many people scared
And others that don't care

They don't consider God
But they pray for more gold

They kill innocent kids
They are acting like wild beasts

They create pollution
And they don't care for a solution

They kill and feel proud
They are an evil crowd

This is called humanity
And I feel embarrassed to be a part of it.

Andreas Christodoulou (13)
The Grammar School, Cyprus

The Beast

The beast, the beast, he's very scary
The beast, the beast, he's too big to carry

The beast, the beast, he's got two black eyes
The beast, the beast, he likes to eat flies

The beast, the beast, his name is Big-Ben
The beast, the beast, he lives in a den

The beast, the beast, he's very furry
The beast, the beast, his vision is blurry

The beast, the beast, he's not so smart
The beast, the beast, he drives a go-kart

The beast, the beast, beware beware
The beast, the beast, he'll give you a scare!

Nik Koukides (13)
The Grammar School, Cyprus

You Died

You died on a Sunday at 4 in the morning
Leaving me mourning all by myself.
You died by yourself, didn't wait for
Anything, didn't wait for anyone.
You died on that terrible Sunday without
Saying bye-bye.
You died, leaving me hoping I'll meet you one day.
You died on a Sunday,
They told me on Monday.
I cried and cried,
I didn't stop crying
I cried by myself
Because you died.

Roxanne Hadjineophytou (12)
The Grammar School, Cyprus

Our World

The world we live today,
Is not the same as yesterday
Half is cruel and bad,
Some is nice and sad.

Some people are evil,
Some people are good,
And poverty is growing,
In this big neighbourhood.

But there is still hope,
That one day,
Wars will stop,
And peace will come by.

Poor will need no help
They will smile and clap,
This was my dream,
And then I woke up.

Leondios Charalambides (12)
The Grammar School, Cyprus

Secrets Of A Love Letter

I have been wandering from hand to hand, hope to hope.
The everlasting lines I have on me are words of love,
Those have been written for her.
My master's hands have longed for love, until she came along.

The unspoken words I have on me are little secrets.
Little secrets of my creator and master of love.

I have been sent from my creator and master of love.
Once I've been sent I must be read.
From the love-the darling, of my creator and master of love.

I'm the hope; I'm the bond of feelings.
Engravings of the deepest love the purest love,
Man can read.

And when I reach my destination, may my master's and creator's
Heart be overwhelmed with fulfilment, achievement in life.
And may his lover's eyes abound with tears of delight.

Through the words I have on me, the proof of eternal love.
For these two souls that shall be bind and never, never be apart.

Kariopouli Demetra (14)
The Grammar School, Cyprus

Peace

Peace is like a dove
Flying in the sky,
Peace is like happiness
To the people all around you.
Peace is like a waterfall
Falling from a hill,
And peace is like when
You get better when you are sick.

Rosemary Alexandrou (12)
The Grammar School, Cyprus

Words

Thanks for words that help me start,
And other words containing art.
Thank you for words that make me greet,
And those bad words like bleed.
Thanks for words that are bitter,
And those other words that are made up of glitter.
Thank you for words that make me go nuts,
And all those other words that give me lots of guts.
Thanks for the words that make my cat kill,
And the words that make my dad cry, 'Not the bill!'
Thanks for words that help me make gangs,
And all those killer words like guns.
Thank you for double words like getting up,
And those disgusting words like throwing up.
Thanks for cool words like matrix,
And my imaginary words like blailix.
Thank you for words like apology,
And words like zoology.
Thanks for words that help me flirt,
(But unfortunately I end up in the dirt!)
Finally, thanks for words that help me end,
(Anyway I have some fruit to blend . . .)

Markos Spyrides (12)
The Grammar School, Cyprus

Global Warming

Winter came but sun is bright
It's only cold at night.
In the day it's mostly hot
What happened? Oh my God!

My reply will be like this:
Global warming! That's what it is!
There is no way to reverse it back,
And now we have to suffer from all that!

Marina Pogosyan (12)
The Grammar School, Cyprus

Prisoners Of Life

Each day seems like one with no sense,
Survival of senseless days is only duty.
As it also is entrapment in a wooden fence,
Only subordination holds the fence, but it will fail.

Rise my fellow inmates!
Let us march together and be rid of control,
Let our freedom blossom from the light of life,
Prisoners of life, ah my dear fellowship don't fail.

Dim light follows us,
For the penalty will be death,
Revolt against life and your future is certain.
Death! It will consume our bright light.

But it is merely a word,
The human will surpass death!
Today all men are independent,
Today no man is blind or deaf.

Women dancing in the chill of night,
Inspiring us to do what is right.
The flames keep on going until night's end,
The aims are still the same.

Sepulchres wait, for we won't be late,
There he is! Having put in the bait.
Jealousy! The weak will fall,
He will take the weak by boat, to Hell.

But the clouds are whiter now, Heaven awaits,
The divine is over us, guiding us.
The Lord from above has destroyed our foe,
Now life has ended without death.

Let us not repeat our mistakes,
Let us not die once more, let us *live!*

Stephanos Chaillou (16)
The Grammar School, Cyprus

Iron Will

Fly, don't await us,
We will just slow you down,
Don't be afraid to impose your own pace.
We will look at you
From the distant past
And admire this creation,
Our experiences and knowledge
Have been passed along to you.
Hopefully, for your help
And when all seems lost,
Like a lighthouse in a pitch-black sea,
We will help you overcome
What may otherwise seem
Impossible for you.
Your rebellious spirit
Has given you
What my rebellious spirit
Has taken from me.
But that doesn't stop me
From being myself
And I am glad
For your happiness.
Hopefully, you will continue
Being who you are.
That ability is the one
Which leads to great success,
A success in all sectors of life.
But what is success
Without the right friends?
Choose them wisely
Because they are rare.
The choosing will be easier
When you are
Yourself.

Daniel Kassabian (15)
The Grammar School, Cyprus

Maria

Maria has blue eyes and blonde hair,
But she is not the king's big heir.
Her cheeks are as red as a rose
And there is a big spot which I think is her nose!

When she is angry, she turns as red as a tomato
And usually breaks everything in the house like a tornado
But she shines us all with her smile when happy
And like a nurse changes the baby's dirty nappy.

She runs like a grey rabbit
And tennis is her big favourite habit.
She eats like a very small mouse
And like a bunny, stays nearly all day in her house!

Georgia Demetriou (12)
The Grammar School, Cyprus

My Prisoner

With silver bracelets,
Wearing black and white,
You wander through my mind,
You hear a sound and follow it,
But you're too scared to leave.
I won't let you, so you stayed,
Wandering alone in my mind.
You walk downhill following a sweet scent,
It's faded but familiar.
You're too scared to leave.
I won't let you so you stayed.
Wandering alone in my mind,
Further down you hear a trembling voice so you follow it.
Balancing on my lips must have been hard while they spoke.
You fell.
Tell me, how does it feel now,
Wandering alone in my heart?

Christianna Orros (16)
The Grammar School, Cyprus

I Loved You Once, I Loved You Twice

I loved you once, I loved you twice,
You trapped my heart and did not hear my sighs.
You made me believe that my beliefs would come true,
But the only belief I had was in you
I wish we could go to Heaven and never come back,
But I just realised that I have bad luck.

I loved you once, I loved you twice,
The day is dark because the sun forgot to rise.
Dark like the night that you left the world,
I wrote 'I love you' with letters in bold.
I missed you yesterday, I miss you today,
But now I know that I miss you every day.

Elina Lemis (12)
The Grammar School, Cyprus

Spring

Spring smells in the east and west
Spring brings hope and zest
Gives us all to calm and rest
Spring is absolutely the best

Springtime is full of blue sky
Butterflies start to fly
Flowers offer their smell with pride
All God's creatures start to smile!

Spring is my loved season
March the child of this season
Gave me my first breath and reason
To live, to experience this season

Spring, you're the year's pleasant king
Blossoms start to dance in a ring
Colours are marching in the fields
And birds sing spring, spring, spring!

Malvina Germanou (13)
The Grammar School, Cyprus

The Argument

Tears of the heart
Make them go away
You shiver them off
The emotions still won't give way

Why all this anger?
Why all this pain?
Aren't we supposed to be happy again?

But what do you mean,
With a stupid 'again'?
Can't even manage
To push the tear down
They're swelling and swelling
They have to get out

What do you do
When your loved one is mad?

What do you do
When they're crazy and sad?

Elina Mantrali (15)
The Grammar School, Cyprus

Orpheas

His eyes are as brown as clay
That helps keep people at bay
He may be as small as a mouse
But his spirit is a house.

At times he's a hog
And can smell like a bog
He can be as sly as a cat
I'd say he's as blind as a bat.

In average he is a regular bloke
He could say the craziest joke
And in the next moment he would seem so sad
Being his friend I'll be always glad.

Niko Gvozdenović (12)
The Grammar School, Cyprus

See The Difference, Make The Difference

Growing up in a world
Full of malice, pain and hatred
Busy people running around
Whatever they do has the same sound

Birds are flying in the sky
I wish I had wings to say goodbye
But there is nothing I can do
I feel too small to make a move

Suddenly a noise wakes me up
I look through the window asking for something to cheer me up
Some children are playing happily in a colourful playground
And a spark starts glowing in my miserable heart

I see that I was wrong for a while
Now the black clouds have been cleared away from the sky
How could I be so pessimistic?
The children are the hope that was missing

A note in a dreamy melody
A brick in the wall
A foundation under a skyscraper
I'm not insignificant at all

We all have to realise the meaning of life
The future is reflected through our own eyes
Young people are the hope of our world
A brighter day will shine and remove the dread

Life is too small to waste it
So we have to find ways to change it
We should never give up and turn our backs
But we should fight, make the difference and join our hands!

Afroditi Karaoli (17)
The Grammar School, Cyprus

The World From The Eyes Of A Poor Fly

Hi! You know who I am?
No, you don't.
I am a poor fly!
I am flying around in your house.
You humans always kill me!
I have a very small life,
I live for 24 hours or . . .
Less!
You don't understand me,
You kill me, but . . .
I haven't done anything to you.
You kill me for no reason,
You have a long life,
But I do not.
You don't respect my life,
You won't let me stay alive,
You kill me sooner,
You have no soul.
Have you ever thought of living so little?
No, of course not!
Have you ever imagined living only for a day?
Have you ever imagined your life this way?
Have you ever thought of being smaller than all others?
Have you ever imagined yourself as a fly?
No!
Because you cannot think about what life means seriously.
Life is to respect others, not kill them,
Life is to respect everyone's life,
Life is to be lived happily,
But you have no brain in your heads!
You kill animals,
You kill insects,
You kill other people,
You destroy your planet,
You have to grow up and . . .
Stop the wars . . .

Don't kill animals,
Don't even kill insects,
Don't dare kill other people,
You have to bring peace to all of the world!
And then . . .
All the problems will be solved.
Only with peace and health comes happiness!
I don't know much
Because . . .
I am a fly,
You humans know more than I!

Andia Phili (14)
The Grammar School, Cyprus

Playing Tennis!

Balls
Not in the halls
Not in the malls
Play in the court with balls . . .
Just play
On the red clay
On this fine day
Not on the bay
Feel yourself feel
Come play ball with me
The vibe is in the air
As the racket blows against your hair
Tennis is cool
And I'd love to say:
The net is not high
So you could play
Tennis, tennis is a pleasure
For me it's a lot of fun,
Give it a try sometime and see,
That tennis is great for you and me!

Dafni Papadopoulou (12)
The Grammar School, Cyprus

The Girl

A small sparrow flies
But it weakens and dies

She did not break his heart
But he broke hers

Now there is no love
No small birds

Lifting her head up high
An icy wind blows, she flies into the night sky

Her eyes shimmer with tears, yet she still flies
Her body is damaged, ready to die

She falls to the earth, but does not care
For her life she does not wish to spare

Her soul weakens, her eyes show pain
Her soul dies, but open her eyes still stay

She dies on a Saturday morning in May
Now her soul sleeps forever, through night and day.

Mark Kazakos (12)
The Grammar School, Cyprus

Alexander (My Brother)

He has eyes like toffee
And hair like coffee
His face is the full moon
I hope you can meet him soon.

A little devil he is some days
His thoughts can be a maze
But then he can be sweet
Just like a sugar beet.

He is a clumsy clown
Like a yo-yo he goes up and down
He is a dolphin in the water
I wish my mum had another daughter!

Eliza Steemers (12)
The Grammar School, Cyprus

Death

A shadow crept
Into a man's shed,
You could see his head
While sleeping in his bed.
He was snoring as loudly as a pig,
The shadow was going to do something big.
What in the world could it be?
It was really a mystery.
The shadow approached the man's bed,
He really seemed to be dead
Because there was something red
Lying next to his own head.
The shadow took out a list
And ticked the man's name,
It really was a beast
Oh, what a shame!
The old man had died
And the shadow took his soul,
The man's face was white
While taken away from our world!

Herodotos Nicolaides (12)
The Grammar School, Cyprus

The Traveller

I'm moving on to walk along
With the birds' song
Near the green leafy trees
I'll be happy and strong.

Nature is so nice
While you watch its sunrise
Life is not so long
So be cheerful and roam.

Annabell Antoniadou (12)
The Grammar School, Cyprus

Food

I hear my tummy
Rumbling
Thumbling
'n' grumbling
Like a violent lion, whose prey will run
A cake six feet high
'n' fish with French fries
Two gazing eyes
And a chicken that flies
My mouth is a desert, fried from the sun
I haven't learnt cooking, since breaking the pan!
A plate with McDonald's
Blueberries with coconuts
Curry from 'Ronald's'
'n' sugar on doughnuts
Sauce and spaghetti
'n' spice like confetti
A 30 ton turkey
A pizza I'm baking
My tummy is
Rumbling
Thumbling 'n' grumbling
Oh why am I reading instead of just eating!

Nastazia Philippou (12)
The Grammar School, Cyprus

Hallowe'en

The moon glows through a hazy mist,
Ghostly headstones by moonlight kissed,
Autumn leaves dead on the ground,
An early frost on a burial mound.

As I walk home this Hallowe'en,
Thinking that I'm alone and unseen,
Chinks of light from the darkness gleam,
Wet leaves of course, or have eyes I seen?

My step I quicken as I look around,
Leaving behind frosty burial mound,
Into the darkness I lengthen my strides,
Feel fear, don't be stupid, nothing here hides.

The street lights have faded,
A cloud shrouds the moon,
The darkness gets darker and darker and dense,
Suddenly it's there! Oh, it's only the fence.

The mist and the darkness have made my eyes blind,
My ears are sure there is someone behind.
Has something escaped from the burial mound?
For it is Hallowe'en, should I be on its ground?

Please let me get home, I won't come here again,
On my own, all alone down this scary old lane:
It's an imaginary journey on which I've just been,
But don't walk in dark places on Hallowe'en.

Charis Theodosiou (12)
The Grammar School, Cyprus

Dreams Vs Reality

I walk down an empty road
I'm surrounded by empty fields
I trudge through an empty life

I look at my home . . .
I see a dead end
A place I must go back to
But I know
I'm walking to a life I don't belong
I look back at what I leave behind
A life I control
Just a few steps behind me

I wear a mask
I try to trick people
But I can't trick myself

My eyes burn
My cheeks are soaked
I can't stay
I want to run
I want to hide
But dead ends surround me

If I go back
I'll wake up to yesterday
Every day is yesterday
I have no tomorrow
I need a way out
I want this life to be mine

I'm a fool
Why do I bother?
Why do I pretend?
My dreams can't become reality

No one understands
No one cares
Trapped!

Trapped in an abyss
It has no end

I try taking control
But I lose it as quickly as I get it
I'm pulled back
Back to reality

I have it all
But it's too far to reach
It's what is near that is holding me back.

Lia Kouloundis (15)
The Grammar School, Cyprus

Shadows Of Death

In the night
It was nearly midnight
My face was white
In the sight
Something crept behind my back
I was sure it was black
In the shadow I saw a sack
Something was ready to attack
The shadow approached me
I couldn't see
If it was real
But I could feel
A light hand
On my back
Stories that are scary
Written my McBeth
Could be real
About shadows of death
Stories that are scary
I'm trying to see if they're real
He has caught me now
Next who should I kill?

Kristina Tomic (12)
The Grammar School, Cyprus

The Mirror

The world is a translucent mirror
Acting on a thought
Which might be reflected back
Or unfortunately get caught

The naïve thought
Passes right through the mirror
But the evil thought
Is sent right back

Every human on Earth
Holds a mirror
Some small
Some huge
But always strong

And when you look at the mirror
And say, 'Oh she's pretty'
Really she is as ugly and evil as
Them and
. . . me

She lives to kill
Them and
. . . me

She is suffering
Like them and
. . . me

The world is bound
To be destroyed

. . . only then will the mirror break.

Aris Antoniades (15)
The Grammar School, Cyprus

The Cup Of Gold

See the ruins of the castles,
Scattered there, in the silver rain,
See the corpses of the soldiers,
Bred to withstand the pain.

Men burn their lives
And fall for the gold,
Swear their kings
The eternal oaths,
Leave their wives,
Their hearts pierced with swords,
To taste the death with their own eyes,
Their lives cut like cords.

Centuries have passed,
But all is just the same,
How many soldiers think they must
Gain the eternal flame?
Their lives shall flicker once,
Like a candlelight flame
And shall they end their journey of life,
All the same . . .

Kings will live
And kings will die,
The taste of gold shall take the knights high,
But no matter how pretty the gold may be,
They shall find death in its glory.

Ekaterina Moiseeva (18)
The Grammar School, Cyprus

Can You Change The World?

I wish I could change the world
I wish I could erase some wars
Some big mistakes
Some mean dark thoughts.

I wish I could stand up for some people
I wish I could help them
In any way, so they could live better now.

I wish I could turn back time
And not make the same mistakes
I wish I could turn back time
And save some lives.

I wish I could change everything
I wish I could make everyone equal
I wish I could do all this
I wish I could change the world

But even though I know I can't
I keep on wishing
I keep on dreaming
That I can change the world
And do all this.

Can you help me change the world?

Claire Ioannou (13)
The Grammar School, Cyprus

Golden Eagle

I am who soars over the mountains
And valleys over big glittering lakes,
Which gleam red in the setting sunshine.
I am who sees best at night and day.
I am who glides over the mountains in the sun
And at night in the dark.
Both of my sharp yellow eyes are like two searchlights,
Focused on the rocky land which stretches under me
To snow-capped mountains and valleys.
I am the one who can fall from the sky so fast
That I am only a blur of brown, the wind billowing behind me.
I can catch myself only from half of a metre over the soil.
I am one of those who may love the mountains.
I am maybe one of those who has a family to love and take care of.

Viktor von Selchow (12)
The International School of Dusseldorf, Germany

Books

I am always reading a book
I just can't help it
Every time I see a cover
I just have to look
Then when I finished reading it
It doesn't really matter
I just flip back to the first page and start over again
Adventure, history and fiction
I've read them all so many times
Paolini, Rowling and Beckman
Are all in my bookcase
But soon there will be a time
When all good books are read
What will happen when that time comes
I don't want to think about it . . .

Victor Onink (11)
The International School of Dusseldorf, Germany

The Never-Ending War

It seems that this war will not end
Many a rule seem to bend
I wait and wonder and cry at night
I only seek friendship
Where I have the right
To be the person I want to be
And not who everyone wants to see
But in this war that will not end
Many a rule seem to bend
I cannot stop it, I will not try
To fight the evil I feel inside
It's too hard, and I know I can't win
I'm changing from somewhere deep within
I'm becoming a monster so full of hate
It scares me to think
That I'm starting to rate
Other people
This is the war that will not end
Many a rule seem to bend
In the social hierarchy of my school
I'm now friends with those who are cool
I'm judging and hurting but crying inside
Because I know I didn't try
I didn't fight and I didn't win
I've changed from somewhere deep within.

Alina Yasis (12)
The International School of Dusseldorf, Germany

Moving

I glanced across the room,
Which was now so silent and bare.
I walked over to where my bed once stood,
But now, there was nothing.
I thought of all the events that had happened in this room,
All of the sleepovers, pillow fights, secret talks,
Would soon be forgotten,
Because I was not coming back.
I peered out the window,
Which I had looked out of every morning,
As the sky turned from black to blue.
I was leaving everything I knew, loved and cared
About behind.
The place I was going,
Would it be like this place?
The place I had grown to love.
In my closet,
I looked around to see if I had left anything behind.
But no, all of my hair dyes, toothpastes and brushes
Had been stripped from the shelves.
I stepped toward the hall,
And took a final glance at what had been mine for so long.
I wanted to cry, but I had no tears left.
And with that,
I turned out the light,
And shut the door.

Lea Foster (11)
The International School of Dusseldorf, Germany

A Tale Of Sorrow

Sit down my dear,
Drink a cup of tea
For the story might cause you a tear.
Once there was a man
Once a girl
Now this of course does not make your head swirl
The boy was rich
Yet the girl poor
And the boy saw her at a door
Into the light
Nevertheless, her parents would not allow
And the girl began to wail
'Oh woe is me!'
But they got married in secret
In midwinter snow
But then the mother saw it for it was a show
And she sent for a witch
To find them
But she was not so evil and did not kill
And instead did something against their will
She sent them to be stars chasing after one another
Therefore if you see a shooting star, it is one of these unfortunate
Souls who want to be with their love forever.

Anastasia Kordomenos (11)
The International School of Dusseldorf, Germany

Turn Back Time

It's my birthday
I open all my presents
Three months pass, and they are all broken
I wish I could turn back time
I want my presents again
Because I know they won't break
This time
I know how to be careful.

Larissa Sutter (11)
The International School of Dusseldorf, Germany

My Biggest Inspiration

She goes to America all alone.
Although she cries she doesn't come home.
When I see her my heart starts thumping.
I run to her, hug her, kiss her.
The happiness to see her after months is endless
And tears do run and smiles do come.
Just to hear her is cool but to see her is awesome
Let's go to the movies, watch a film, go shopping
But soon the fun is over and tears are running.
Thank you for all you've done for me and I hope now
I can do it for you.

It's my turn,
Philly.

Camilla Brenninkmeyer (12)
The International School of Dusseldorf, Germany

Glue Called Love

I open my book of experience,
Of laughter and joy,
Of bad things and sad things,
And tears of joy.

I open the page of Thursday the third.
So long and full.
I noticed a hole,
A hole in my heart,
That hole grew bigger
And healed when I met you.

You were the one who fixed my heart with your glue.
The glue called love.

Mans Rosberg (12)
The International School of Dusseldorf, Germany

Turn Back Time

Me and Dad
At the big parade
I was cold and sick
My dad told me to go home.
But I didn't want to go home,
Why should I go home?
It was no use.
After the parade, I wasn't brave!
I got really sick. I got a serious cold.
Staying in my bed for two weeks,
Taking medicines every hour.
What a boring time!
In my bed I was sure that
He was right, and I was wrong
I think that I might be better
To do what he says!

Martin Bruhat (12)
The International School of Dusseldorf, Germany

Ice Skating

Twisting, turning, sliding around
One jump up then falling down
Circles and circles
Rounds and rounds
On one leg
Faster, faster
Then a big bow
There I was in the middle of the ice
Getting applause and the first prize.

Amelie Blomeyer (11)
The International School of Dusseldorf, Germany

Star

I am a star
I live so far away from you

I am in the sky
With others nearby

When I shoot
I saw your suit

I don't know why
But I sit here and cry

I feel so lonely without my friends
I send them wind-messages

I hope I see you
One day or another

Goodbye.

Elijah Nicholson (11)
The International School of Dusseldorf, Germany

My Guitar

Glossy, smooth, cherry-red surface
Strong, fine strings glistening as they catch the light
Ready and waiting for the magic moment
When it will come alive
Responding to the mood of the player
Changing from a fat friendly contented child to a
Heavy, hard, clear and confident Harley Davidson biker.
My guitar.

Alexander Haub (12)
The International School of Dusseldorf, Germany

Through The Eyes Of A Book

There are many places where I can be found,
I'm one of the best resources around,
I can be big, small, thick or thin,
My pages are my body, my cover is my skin,
I come in different categories to suit people's taste,
Although some people prefer to look at me in haste,
Much interest in me has started to fade,
Some don't care if I was or wasn't made,
I'm nothing like a television set,
I provide more education, that's a sure bet,
I give more than just bare facts to see,
I give opinions, ideas that people can find out through me,
But technology's increasing, so all interest in me may soon be gone,
But no matter how good the technology is, I can show you the world,
And the world's beyond,
Because the world is shown by the people who made me,
So if you want to see through those people's eyes then use me,
Now that you've seen through me, take a closer look,
Because my real identity is none other than a book.

Gabi Fagen (12)
The International School of Dusseldorf, Germany

Samiko

My sister screams a lot
She always annoys me
Teasing, kicking, killing
Anyway she can annoy me
Is she really family?
I don't think so
But when I asked my mum she says
She is our family
My sister always annoys me
I'm getting a headache . . .

Toma Takahashi (12)
The International School of Dusseldorf, Germany

More Than Just A Possibility

Far away as it may seem,
Anything can happen if you follow your dream.
Put your mind to it and try.
Spread your wings and you can fly.
Just ignore what others say,
Believe in yourself and go your own way.
Whatever your dream may be,
Open your eyes and you will see
That confidence is the key.
Calm down and just be free.
Remember that no one can make your wishes come true
Except for you.

Bridget Kenion (11)
The International School of Dusseldorf, Germany

When I Fly

When I fly high in the sky
Time just seems to pass me by

Flipping, soaring, turning, diving
I can do all this without even trying

Seeing people down below
Squirrels, chipmunks, deer and does

Climbing high above the clouds
Hearing all the city sounds

Seeing the world from a high up view
Wish that you all could see it too

I am a bird high in the sky
This is what I do when I fly.

Megan McCormick (11)
The International School of Dusseldorf, Germany

For The Future And This Planet Please Take Care Of Me!

I travel around everywhere,
Even in the human body,
I can be clean or dirty,
But nothing can live without me.

Everything alive I make it survive,
I come from the rain, the snow and the dew,
You can find me anywhere.

I am clear and I have no taste,
I'm in every house in Dusseldorf,
I can be dirty or clean depending on the way you treat me.

I am water,
That most people drink every day,
Nobody can live without me,
But everybody's polluting me,
And many people are starting to get ill,
Just because many people make me dirty when they shouldn't.

Please don't waste me,
Because I'm valuable to you,
I am one of the basic needs to everybody.

I beg you to take care of me,
Before the time runs out and it's too late,
I'm depending on everybody,
For the future and this planet.

Yeon Soo Kim (11)
The International School of Dusseldorf, Germany

Time

Time flies,
Unpredictable for its size.
The ticking of the clock makes me think,
How fast ships can sink.

Time flies,
Just like the throwing of a die.

You can never tell the future,
As it is already under torture of time.
The future is a hidden secret.
Time is the heart of the world.
It connects physical things such as you,
And the central heartbeat of the world.
It keeps everything so rhyming.

Time,
Gives apples their red,
The sun a yellow colour,
And everything else,
Its own unique colour.
It is as powerful like a drunken bull,
And yet so gently ticking.

Time,
Keeps everything so rhyming.

Jan Sokol (12)
The International School of Dusseldorf, Germany

Lonely

You hear a raindrop falling in a puddle.
You don't feel anything, you feel nothing.
But when you look up you find a smiling face
And all of a sudden you feel happy.
Now you're not a nobody, you are someone.
Don't worry, be brave, you'll find a friend.
Because friendship will never end.
Friendship!

Constance Valette (11)
The International School of Dusseldorf, Germany

Why Am I So Different?

They laughed and kicked
She could feel her skin get ripped

She would never say a word
She would never show her fears

How could those with cold heart be worthy of her tears?
She promised herself to not show them her real feelings
To show them her tears was her ultimate fear

She screamed on the inside
But no one could hear
No one would care

She would let it all out by screaming in the rain
But the sound would fade away along with the pain

Who could she ask for help?
No one would understand

Understand that the people that seemed to be her friends
They were the people against whom she couldn't defend

They laughed and kicked
Suddenly her fear slipped

She tried to keep it back for she knew she could be strong
But the fear she kept in for so long came all along

One of them looked into her eyes
And she into his
She knew she could no longer take all of this

Tears rolling down her soft but cold cheeks
Falling to the ground gently and swift
She started to shiver because she had done wrong
She had promised herself that they were not worthy of her tears all
Along

She closed her eyes and tried to see beyond
All the terrible things they to her did wrong

They laughed and kicked
She could feel her heart get ripped

Ripped into pieces by kids in her age
All she did was be different from them.

Anna Ström (15)
The International School of Naples, Italy

Deep Minds

It is the truth, it is a lie
Am I cruel or can I fly?

I feel it here, I feel it there
Is it the heart, the centre of everywhere?

Cheaper and cheaper it gets per time
But is it worth the same for mine?

I feel like a lonely boy in the deep forest
Can the power of love be so enormous?

I will search and find it
But what if again I get so blinded?

Use your life, do not throw it away
Because now is now and we live today.

Niklas Anspach (15)
The International School of Naples, Italy

. . . Torn . . .

And today is the day that I let you go.
Today is the day, it's time for you to know.
I let you break me, and tear me down.
Now I'm stronger, since you're not around.

But please don't cry . . .
I just have to do what I think is right.

Maybe in the future, things could get better
But I don't see that, not now . . . not ever.
You can tell yourself that I'm coming back,
But your wishes won't change what happened in the past.

So please don't cry . . .
I just have to do what I think is right.
And it's our time,
Cos sooner or later,
We all have to learn to let go.

In the darkness, in the snow . . .
I don't need you anymore.
Through the lightning, through the storm . . .
I don't need you anymore.

I'm finding my way home,
And I have to do this alone.
Because when you're near,
My happiness turns into tears.

And maybe it's just fear,
Afraid to get too close . . . too near.
Stranded in the darkness,
Isolated by my tears.
But maybe we can't let go.
Maybe that's not the way,
But how do we know.

Torn between my feelings for you,
I just wish we could start anew.

Bianca Allen (14)
The International School of Naples, Italy

The Meaning Of Life

First paint a dark hole,
With a shadow,
Lightly stroking the floor,
Then paint a crack,
A shaft of sunlight,
A layer of dust,
A pebble washed up by the waves.

The waves,
Hear the rushing, roaring,
Gentle whispering,
Feel the sharpness of the spray,
See the treasures it captures,
Then frees.

Wait and watch,
For a second, month, year or even ten lifetimes,
Wait,
Then you might see,
If you have the eyes keen enough,
A world unexplored by man,
Crabs, fish, stones,
Paint them all, then,

Put down the brush,
Put down the canvas,
Touch a small grain of history,
Slip it in your pocket,
Leave.

That small piece of material has captured,
Captured the meaning of life.

Olivia Favis (11)
Windsor School, Germany

What Is Money To You?

Money,
Could be a comfy bed to sleep in at night.
Money,
Could be new Xbox 360 to play.
Money,
Could be knowing if you'll get food tonight.
Money,
Could be somewhere warm to stay.
Money
Could help you have a healthy life.
Money,
Could be a warm coat to wear in the cold.
Money,
Could be a place to sleep at night.
Money,
Could be someone to look after you when you're old,
Money,
Could be a roof over your head,
Money,
You can't take it with you when you're dead.

Amina Fiaz (12)
Windsor School, Germany

Skiing

The sound of my skis fighting mounds of thick snow,
The freezing wind reddening my face.
Whizzing downhill I shout as I go,
Plummeting down in my own little race.

Adrenaline rushes as I build up great speed,
Snaking through slopes narrow and wide
Reaching inside for the courage I need,
Exhausted and exhilarated at the end of the ride.

Esme Howard (11)
Windsor School, Germany

I Wonder If

I wonder if I were good, would I be praised?
I wonder if I were good, would I get more friends?
I wonder if we would fly, I would fly up to the sky.
Would it be fun or would I die?
Should I be happy or should I cry?
I wonder if I was a fish, could I swim from sea to sea?
Would it be fun or would a shark eat me for its tea?
I wonder if there was a you and me,
If there was, together we could sail the seven seas
I wonder if you are not there, I guess it will just be me.
I wonder if you were a star, would you be loved more than you
already are?
I wonder if you were mean, would it be hard for me?

Elle Whelan (11)
Windsor School, Germany

My Hero

My hero has lived with me my whole life,
My hero wears a uniform with pride,
My hero has been to Afghanistan,
My hero is very funny sometimes,
My hero can do stuff I can't,
My hero is my teacher of life,
My hero helps me,
My hero made me,
My hero has done things I have yet to do,
My hero has travelled,
My hero can spell (I can't)
My hero has been places I haven't,
My hero has seen things I haven't,
So who is my here?
My dad!

Kyle Hadnett (13)
Windsor School, Germany

If I Could

If I could turn back time,
And do it all again,
I wouldn't have a fight with
My best friend Ben.

I'd tell him I was sorry,
And I wish I hadn't done
The terrible things I did to him
Just for my pure fun.

I wish I hadn't kicked him
Pulled and clenched his hair,
I wish I could've hidden
In my private, secret lair

He cried and wept as if he had
Lost a special person
And throughout the day his nasty wounds,
They began to worsen.

I wish I hadn't done that,
I knew that it was wrong
And if time loved me very much
I'd say, 'I wish that fight was gone.'

Emily Moseley (12)
Windsor School, Germany

War Is Wrong!

Across the dusty fields of dew,
Are the glittering waves of petal-blue.
Where battleships once risked their fate,
To restore our freedom till this date.
This war was endless, quite untold,
Yet like a journal to unfold . . .

Our soldiers fought back at last,
This warped us to our gloomy past.
Pacing pants of Germans fled,
As bullets in their bodies bled.

This is wrong when we think back,
To see us fighting, war is black.
This could happen at anytime,
Even when I end this rhyme.

Across the dusty fields of dew,
Are the glittering waves of petal-blue.
Where battleships once risked their fate,
To restore our freedom till this date.

Scott Carson (11)
Windsor School, Germany

An Extraordinary Being

The sun beamed into the house
And shone on his wings
The wings that were pure white
And spread out from his shoulder blades
As he got up and stretched
He was as tall as a fully grown man
And his wings stretched right out and filled the room
He turned and saw the birds fly through the sky
And wished he could be like them
They flew past with their wings spread out and their beaks stuck out
As if they were trying to catch something.
They flew on past the shining sun and through the blue sky.
He stepped outside and looked in the sky
Closed his eyes and wished so hard that he drifted off up, up and up
He had done it he was flying
All of the birds joined him as they flew over the houses and factories
Loving every moment of it
An extraordinary being.

Jasmine Wilson (11)
Windsor School, Germany

Rose

While a white rose swayed in the wind
We watched in awe,
As the flattering silver petals opened,
Into a sight to remember,
Take a picture,
And look back at the sight you saw,
A rose,
Showing its inner body,
Oh how lucky!
Remember, wild roses, old garden roses or Alba,
Are as beautiful as the sunshine,
Growing old.

Joshua Haigh (12)
Windsor School, Germany

I Wonder . . .

I wonder what would have happened that day,
If I hadn't have cheered them on.
I wouldn't have got caught up in the fight,
And the hate would long since have gone.

I wonder what they are doing right now,
I wonder what they would say,
If I turned up on their doorstep,
And tried to apologise one day.

I wonder what I should do,
Now that has passed away.
Should I go and apologise,
Or keep my life this way?

Annie Fidler (12)
Windsor School, Germany

Dreams

I dreamt upon a stormy night
A beautiful dream of fright and flight,
I dreamt that I boarded a plane
And dreamt I was never seen again.

The flight was called 101
It went down in a thunderstorm,
It all happened on a Sunday morn
I dreamt I was newly born.

The engines were struck by lightning
Suddenly my dream became very frightening,
I woke up in the middle of the night
Then found out I was alright.

Michael Maguire (13)
Windsor School, Germany

Your Name Is Too Dear
(To Speak Above A Whisper)

(For my grandad, whose legacy will forever live within the family he cared for)

You had to leave us
You had to leave me,
You're not here now
You're just a memory,
I had a choice;
To see you one more time,
I was alone with you
That time was mine,
I held your hand
And whispered in your ear
Those words I said
I knew you could hear.

We sat around you
And we watched you breathe,
We sat around you,
And watched your life unweave,
Your last breath
Set your place in our hearts,
With you gone
Another life starts,
A loving husband
With a name too dear,
A caring father,
All reflected, in a single tear.

Daryl Aitken (17)
Windsor School, Germany

Young Writers Information

We hope you have enjoyed reading this book - and that you will continue to enjoy it in the coming years.

If you like reading and writing poetry drop us a line, or give us a call, and we'll send you a free information pack.

Alternatively if you would like to order further copies of this book or any of our other titles, then please give us a call or log onto our website at www.youngwriters.co.uk

**Young Writers Information
Remus House
Coltsfoot Drive
Peterborough
PE2 9JX**

(01733) 890066